COLLECTED WORKS OF
CHARLES BAUDOUIN

Volume 6

THE MYTH OF MODERNITY

THE MYTH OF MODERNITY

CHARLES BAUDOUIN

Translated by
BERNARD MIALL

LONDON AND NEW YORK

First published in 1950

This edition first published in 2015
by Routledge
27 Church Road, Hove BN3 2FA

and by Routledge
711 Third Avenue, New York, NY 10017

Routledge is an imprint of the Taylor & Francis Group, an informa business

© 1950 Charles Baudouin

All rights reserved. No part of this book may be reprinted or reproduced or utilised in any form or by any electronic, mechanical, or other means, now known or hereafter invented, including photocopying and recording, or in any information storage or retrieval system, without permission in writing from the publishers.

Trademark notice: Product or corporate names may be trademarks or registered trademarks, and are used only for identification and explanation without intent to infringe.

British Library Cataloguing in Publication Data
A catalogue record for this book is available from the British Library

ISBN: 978-1-138-82541-3 (Set)
eISBN: 978-1-315-73901-4 (Set)
ISBN: 978-1-138-82654-0 (Volume 6)
eISBN: 978-1-315-73902-1 (Volume 6)

Publisher's Note
The publisher has gone to great lengths to ensure the quality of this reprint but points out that some imperfections in the original copies may be apparent.

Disclaimer
The publisher has made every effort to trace copyright holders and would welcome correspondence from those they have been unable to trace.

CHARLES BAUDOUIN

THE MYTH OF MODERNITY

TRANSLATED BY
BERNARD MIALL

LONDON
GEORGE ALLEN & UNWIN LTD

FIRST PUBLISHED IN 1950

This book is copyright under the Berne Convention. No portion may be reproduced by any process without written permission. Inquiries should be addressed to the publishers.

The original of this work is
LE MYTHE DU MODERNE
published by Les Editions du Mont-Blanc, Geneva, in the Collection Action et Pensée

PRINTED IN GREAT BRITAIN
in 12-*point Bembo type*
BY THE BLACKFRIARS PRESS LTD
LEICESTER

CONTENTS

		Page
I.	From the Myth of Progress to the Myth of Modernity	1
II.	The Clean Sweep	10
III.	Angelism	23
IV.	Politeness	28
V.	Technique versus Nature	36
VI.	Baudelaire and the Modern Man	51
VII.	Of the Prestige of Action	56
VIII.	Communions	60
IX.	Opinion and Tolerance	65
X.	Humanism	76
XI.	Eloquence on Trial	81
XII.	Of Reading	89
XIII.	Technique versus Mysticism	95
XIV.	A Moderate View of Happiness	99
XV.	The Paradoxes of Education	115
XVI.	The Gift of Childhood	121
XVII.	Confidence in Mankind	128
XVIII.	An Apology for the Unruly	136
XIX.	Withdrawal into one's Tent	146
XX.	Verlaine	149
XXI.	Art and the Epoch	157

I
FROM THE MYTH OF PROGRESS TO THE MYTH OF MODERNITY

I

THE last two centuries were familiar with the myth of Progress. Our own century has adopted the myth of Modernity. The one myth has replaced the other.

II

It was by gradual transitions—almost by sleight of hand—that the myth of Progress was transformed into that of Modernity. So true is this that the second myth is still often expressed in the language of the first, whereby people are deceived. But the tone of the myth is different, and the words in which it is expressed have a different meaning.

III

Let us try to follow these transitions : Belief in Progress saw a better world in the future ; hence it was good to make haste toward the future ; hence the prestige of change, and of speed. Belief in Progress beheld in science, and the techniques which science introduces, its most trustworthy instrument ; hence the prestige of the machine. And then, as will happen, the end was forgotten even as one approached it ; the means became an end in themselves. Speed and the machine are among the principal elements of the new myth. As speed is a product of the machine, and as, moreover, both speed and the machine are modern conquests, these three entities : speed, machinery, and modernity, are immediately associated in a single closely-knit complex.

IV

Thus, the modern myth is the myth of *Modernity*. Yet all

bygone epochs, you may say, were modern in their time. But this is not true. Our epoch has invented the trick of glorying in the fact of its own existence. Modernity's way of priding itself on its modernity is entirely modern. What has been called "the end of eternity" is precisely the reverse.

V

Once our aim was "progress". Why was that aim abandoned as we journeyed on ? It had claimed to be, amongst other things, moral progress. But this was a claim that could not be upheld. The war of 1914, very perceptibly, struck it a formidable blow. And what of the war of 1939 ? Men ceased to believe in progress; but only to pin their faith to more tangible realities, whose sole original significance had been that they were the instruments of progress.

VI

People began to contemn the naïveté of a belief in progress. But is it not equally naïve to boast, as though it were meritorious, of the fact that one is bringing up the rear ?

VII

Moreover, this exaltation of the present (not so much because it is the present as because it is something new) is a corollary of that very faith in progress which people claim to have discarded. The present is superior to the past, by definition, only in a mythology of progress. Thus one retains the corollary while rejecting the principle. There is only one way of retaining a position of whose instability one is conscious. One must simply refrain from thinking—and surrender oneself to the vortex of the corollary. And then speed comes to our aid.

VIII

But every speed may be exceeded ; every machine improved. Will not the vortex end by plunging into the abyss ? For everywhere the myth of modernity results in rising costs, in inflation.

FROM THE MYTH OF PROGRESS TO THE MYTH OF MODERNITY

IX

In a mythology of Progress humanity has its aspirations, and the term "ideal" has a meaning. In a mythology of Modernity humanity seems rather to be fleeing before a pursuer. In the first case the value of the passing moment is measured by the decreasing distance from the end to be attained; in the second case there is no end; the value of the passing moment is measured by *records*, by comparison with previous moments; the most a man can do is incessantly to flee from the past, which he feels always at his heels. The heel is the vulnerable spot of this Achilles. And before him he sees nothing—not even the tortoise.

X

The myth of Progress gives humanity reasons to aspire to better things; reasons for happiness; inasmuch as the man who aspires is a happy man. The myth of Modernity seems to give humanity reasons for fleeing from itself; reasons for unhappiness, inasmuch as the man who runs away from himself is an unhappy man.

XI

Aristocratic spirits, in the nineteenth century, were rather inclined to fall foul of the myth of Progress; they felt that it savoured of beer and skittles. But if Progress is "democratic," Modernity is vulgar. It savours less of the people than of the *parvenu*, the *nouveau riche*. Are not persons of distinction beginning to resent the description of "modern" as an insult?

XII

However, the contrast between the "people" and the parvenu is tending to become less obvious. In proportion as it accepts the myth of Modernity the "people" no longer behave like "the people", but like the parvenu. One can always be a parvenu in respect of someone—even if that someone be merely oneself. A really modern man of the people prides himself less on the possession of the right to vote than on the possession of a motor-car or a bathroom. A certain contempt for "modern comfort" becomes, by a sort of rebound, a mark of distinction.

THE MYTH OF MODERNITY

XIII

People speak of "the crisis of democracy". We should ask whether democracy is not losing ground in the same proportion as the myth of Progress. And we should reflect on the parallelism of these three phenomena: the substitution of Modernity for Progress, of the record for the ideal, of the philosophy of dictatorships for the ideology of democracy.

XIV

Even if there is a democratic crisis it does not follow that the crisis will facilitate a return to aristocracy and distinction.

XV

The vulgarity of the myth of Modernity is plainly revealed by the pre-eminence in its mythology of the factors of quantity; to be modern is always to "beat the record" in some respect. Distinction, therefore, is opposed to modernity as quality is to quantity. Moreover, the "modern" man ingenuously confesses that he tends toward the "standard"—that is, toward uniformity; the very reverse of distinction.

XVI

Those who reproach the myth of Progress for its lack of aristocratic distinction do not perceive that the myth of Modernity is even more lacking in this respect.

XVII

The "modern" man sees through the illusions of Progress; but he does not see through the illusions of Modernity; since for Modernity he has a passion; and in it he has his being. But it may be that the illusions of Modernity are the grosser and the more pernicious. And is not the most pernicious feature in the myth of Progress the fact that it prepares the way for the myth of Modernity?

XVIII

The tragedy of the modern man is that his civilization has begun to decline at the very moment when, persuaded by the faith of the last few centuries, he was on the point of conceiving and adopting a belief in Progress. Then, proceeding from the postulate that in order to progress he had only to go forward with the times, and that any change must be an improvement, he was bound to regard even the first movements on the downward path as progress ; and thus he was fated to hasten them, and go distractedly to his downfall.

XIX

The Disputed Passage, by Lloyd G. Douglas, brings together, at a certain moment, a Chinaman, Abott, and an American, Beaven, who begin to strike up a friendship. One day Abott appears with a basket containing all the ingredients for a stew, and he proves to be an excellent cook ; nevertheless, while he busies himself with his stewpan he finds time to discuss various subjects of importance with Beaven, who is perched on a stool.

The Chinaman asserts that in his country people are content with things as they are, whereas the Americans are eager for change. And in fact the word "change" elicits an immediate response from Beaven. Of course, he says, in effect, there must be changes if there is to be progress ; indeed, he would go so far as to say that whenever there is change there is progress ; that was his natural, his congenital conviction.

But the Chinaman looks up with a sceptical smile. He is much more inclined to believe that the things which pride themselves on being progressive are merely immaterial changes. He sums up his philosophy in a sentence : "What is gained on the one hand is lost on the other." And he says further : "It may be that a dozen lives were saved today in Michigan by new methods of surgery. As many have been lost through the invention of the motor-car. Aviation enables big business men to complete their operations more rapidly. But it also provides us with a new

engine of destruction. And destruction doesn't improve matters."
We had already encountered similar ideas; not only on studying the *Tao*, but also on hearing what Emerson had to tell us of compensation; so that in spite of the antithesis of the foregoing dialogue, the American may after all come to the Chinaman's way of thinking.

XX

There is, in the *Bréviaire* of Armand Godoy, a *Prayer for the Departed*. I should like to take from this one vigorous stanza; it was surely dedicated to the men of our own day:

Ah, leur raison, triste machine délabrée,
Torturant l'arbre afin d'avoir plus tôt son fruit,
Creusant des trous dans l'Étendue et la Durée,
Pour les boucher avec les cendres de l'Ennui !

The first of men did no more than take the fruit of the tree, and that, we are told, was Sin. Modern humanity "tortures the tree in order the sooner to obtain its fruit," which is vice rather than sin, for it is contrary to nature. It gives way to impatience; it kills the goose that lays the golden eggs.

It is "torturing the tree" when we overwork ourselves as the pace of modern life almost inevitably condemns us to do, when we proudly speed through "holes in the air" in order to gain time, as we say. But having gained this time, what do we do with it? We don't know what to do with it, save to waste it. We reverse the method of Proust; *A la recherche de la perte du temps gagné !* We seek to recover the wasted time that we have gained ! And to this end we invent the most idiotic pastimes. But we do not gain our end: we are left with ennui, and the taste of its ashes remains with us. Perhaps we could do better, but we should have to go right back to the beginning, to listen to the wisdom of the tree, to attune our rhythm to the rhythm of flowering and ripening.

XXI

There is something morbid and neurotic in the revolt against the laws of life. The man of harmonious nature accepts the seasons of life as he accepts the hours of the day; he accepts the coming of old age with serenity—and here the word has its true meaning: the calm of evening. With this serenity he goes onward to death itself.

The desire to remain young at any cost, which really ends in a ridiculous aping of youth, is one of the symptoms of the modern neurosis. The result is pitiable. It has been trenchantly described by the psycho-analyst Edouard Pichon: Compare, he says, that delightful person, a grandmother, with that ridiculous object: an old photograph.

But first of all, the former lived. René Cellendy has said, in effect, that those who have known how to love know how to die; in which saying he condenses his experience as a psychologist and a medical practitioner. He brings us a little farther.

When we say that in order to know how to grow old and to die one must have lived, we may not be understood. It might be thought that he does not regret his life who has known how to profit by it, to *take* much, and who is therefore, so to speak, satiated. But this is not so; it is almost the reverse of the truth. To have lived a full life is to have learned to love, that is, to *give* greatly. It is to have learned how to make the gesture that some scholars have called *oblative*, opposing this term to *captative*; as though contrasting the gesture of offering with the gesture of seizure. It is to have learned that we possess nothing of our own; that we ought to be able to surrender everything with a good grace; giving ourselves to our descendants, to a group which contains us, to an idea which surpasses us. At the end of this apprenticeship death appears no more than the supreme offering and restitution.

XXII

An amiable lady, who some little time ago took to riding a bicycle, told me, with a smile: "Once you are on wheels and have the road beneath you the notion of truth becomes a little vague. One had hoped one was too honest for that. But now, to begin with, one thinks only of deceiving the police, and one lies as smoothly as one bowls along the road." Was this merely a jest ? If one recalls the myth of Mercury, who flies with wings at his heels, and is at once the god of speed and the god of thieves, one may come to believe that the fair cyclist's confession was nearer the truth than one had supposed. As a matter of fact, there are wits who find honesty a trifle pedestrian, a little provincial and peasant-like ; and one speaks of easy morals : *moeurs légères*. Can it be true that whatever gives us wings delivers us from earnestness ? And are we to think that the "holidays from probity" recently denounced by Claparéde are not unrelated to the use of rapid vehicles, which make us the devotees of Mercury ?

When one seems to have grown lighter, when one travels quickly, one is inclined to "make a get-away," the temptation is so strong ! The love of risk plays its part. And if it is true that the fear of the policeman is the beginning of wisdom, then wisdom is sadly endangered by the prospect and the pleasure of flight.

But there is more to be said on this subject. Honesty is based on a contract, and the contract, in its turn, is essentially a guarantee of stability. It brings matters to a standstill, and says, thus they shall remain. In the same spirit one speaks of a legal settlement, which tells us plainly enough that obedience to the law goes hand-in-hand with immobility. In the army is not the first word of command the *garde-à-vous* ? Stand at attention ! And every promise is the magnificent attempt of man to put fetters on time, to immobilize the flux of things. And truth, in its turn, is related to obedience, to the sworn oath. It "affirms" ; which is to say, it holds fast. It supposes that this is that, that this equals that, and thus takes it for granted that the first of these terms has not undergone a change even while it was being identified with the second. What will you venture to affirm of a landscape swept by the wind of speed, which speed demolishes at every moment ? Truth has no longer time to be born.

Hugo foresaw a magnificent future for humanity endowed with

FROM THE MYTH OF PROGRESS TO THE MYTH OF MODERNITY

wings. Delivered of weight, it would be utterly free ; for "this chain was all chains." There is reason to fear that of all the fetters which the devotee of Mercury will be tempted to discard the first may be those of truth and honesty. It must be admitted that it is not very healthy for a man to go too fast.

II
THE CLEAN SWEEP

I

THE interplay of action and reaction is one of the laws of life; which, like an infallible instinct, wiser than we, restores in us an equilibrium which we exercize our ingenuity in destroying.

This interplay of natural compensations explains to some extent the variations of taste, less capricious than they might seem to be. One understands, of course, that one period likes to differ from the period that preceded it, asserting itself against it as a son asserts himself against his father. But there are many different ways of differing and asserting oneself, and the choice of the way adopted is not left to chance. Thus the modern taste in architecture, and in the various forms of decoration, tends without question to bareness, simplification, the elimination of fussy ornament. And it is obvious, of course, that in this one is reacting against the abuse of ornament and the over-elaborate style of a previous period; when, moreover, the anxiety to decorate everything at all costs, while making articles quickly and cheaply, by mass production, had resulted in an invasion of commonplace and tasteless decorations. But this is not all.

The modern man hankers after sensation; he cannot have too much of it. Our rapid means of transport and information enable him to gratify this taste to satiety. Satiety: that is the operative word. The modern man is tired, when the evening comes, by all the things he has caused to dance before his eyes all day, by means of the motor-car or the cinema; by all that has been filling his ears and his head with the confusion of a bazaar and a world exposition. It is then that he likes to find, in his home, in the familiar objects which he has to handle, a quality of repose. Let these things be smooth and simple, smooth as soap, to cleanse him from the dust of the outer world that is clinging to him. They must liberate him from the dancing, jigging turmoil of the day. Hence a taste for straight, simple lines, without surprises; for bare surfaces, for carpets without patterns, for walls without pictures; hence an instinctive attempt to purge the senses after the surfeit of sensations with which he has deliberately gorged himself. He is dieting himself after an orgy.

Wisdom will object that he would have done better to refrain from these excesses. But the instruments by which he multiplies his sensations are novelties; and the modern man plays with them as a savage plays with his glass beads; he does not know how to make judicious use of them. And then, the solicitations are so urgent and so perpetual, like the dance of the neon lights in a busy street.

It will be a problem, for the man of tomorrow, to school himself to limiting his excursions in the world of sensation, which has become too accessible; to take only as much as he can tolerate. In the meantime it would be wiser to refrain from pluming ourselves on this longing for bare surfaces, devoid of all decoration, as the acme of good taste, for it is, in actual fact, merely the first expression of disgust!

II

Despite the prudent truism that one should not argue about tastes and colours, such a discussion, when one does indulge in it, proves to be highly instructive. For questions of taste immediately lead one to wider issues; and the most profound disagreements as to matters of taste converge (so that prudence, from its own point of view, may very well hesitate to thrust a stick into the anthill!).

We have envisaged the modern taste for simplification as a reaction against the excess of sensations in respect of which the modern man has become a sort of pincushion. But it may be that this reaction of creating a vacuum goes farther than we realize.

We shall see that this taste for making a clean sweep very

THE MYTH OF MODERNITY

quickly assumes an aggressive and destructive form. We have only to recall the sally emitted during the Second Empire by Rochefort's *Lanterne*, with reference to the new boulevards of Hausmann, which cut their way through the jungle of little crooked lanes : "The straight line is the machine-gun's shortest way to the barricade." To simplify up to a certain point is the next thing to hacking down. To restore order, to clean things up, we scrap them, we burn them, and there is an instinct that takes a certain pleasure in so doing. It must be admitted that in the modern liking for the clean sweep there is a trace of this pleasure—should we say, of this sadism ? It is enough to reflect on the manner in which our cities are treated under the pretext of improving them and making them healthier. In certain hands this operation is almost as effective as bombardment from the air.

And since the word has been spoken, we cannot refrain from asking whether the wholesale devastations of modern war do not themselves respond to a certain instinct, a certain impulse, of the clean sweep. May they not be, in the last analysis, related to the taste, which seems to be so utterly innocent, for blank surfaces and rooms without knick-knacks and curios ? May they not be, in a sense, the exorbitant and apocalyptic magnification of what originally appeared a mere aesthetic preference ? I believe people are beginning to realize that the so-called modern spirit is to an alarming degree a spirit of destruction. Has humanity, confronted by an excess of riches, too easily obtained, ended by regarding them with nausea, until it longs to destroy them in a sort of frenzy, a passion for the clean sweep ? One could almost believe it.

Yes, it is true—it is better not to argue about tastes and colours . . .

III

This craving for simplification, this impulse to clear the ground, reveals itself also in the order of ideas, and here the result is somewhat disappointing. We have libraries, a superabundance of books, reviews, and newspapers, on which an incredible wealth of talent is expended, and in which works and articles of real excellence are not rare ; we have the documentary and illustrative film, and, last but not least, we have the radio. But have we derived the benefit that we have a right to expect from all these admirable mediums ? Have we increased our intellectual pleasures, our knowledge of the world, our wisdom, in short, in proportion to the progress of these mediums ? It is only too plain that we have not. Indeed, the answer sometimes given to this question is : "On the contrary"—and not always by the pessimist. The average culture of today seems inferior to that of yesterday. The intelligence of the man in the street seems to have lost, not gained, in variety and subtlety. And the schoolmasters are always telling us that in the last twenty-five years the level of their classes has declined to a disquieting degree. Now, this quarter-century is precisely that which has enriched us with so many improvements in our means of tuning in to the universe.

How can we explain this disappointing result ? It is due, no doubt, to a number of causes. But one of these can be isolated ; it is, once more, the fatigue, the species of nausea, that results from excess ; the taste for the "clean sweep" as a defensive reaction against congestion. Just as we no longer want ornaments and bric-à-brac ; just as we hack our way through our cities and massacre the riches of Nature at the very time when these were becoming accessible in abundance, so we no longer covet the ornaments of the mind, and reject the intellectual riches that press upon us from every side. And this is a serious matter. The taste for the slogan, for the straightforward, ready-made thought, which does not compel us to think, is a phenomenon of the same order. Here again, as in the decorative arts and elsewhere, we are making a clearance. But here again, without discernment. And at this trivial game we run the risk of stultifying ourselves, of being once again "defeated by our conquest." The problem is one of the right degree, but this we shall not find without a search. The reaction of the moment does not search for the proper degree; it is instinctive and brutal. Here again, the reaction is sane enough in principle. And the barbarism is healthy ; but the barbarian is still a barbarian.

IV

The modern man—we observed—is multiplying his sensations to the point of distraction. But it soon appears that he becomes his own dupe. Not only is he quickly wearied, as we have seen ; seeking only to find repose in stripping himself bare. But the readjustment has not even waited for him to do so before coming into play. It may be detected at every step of his frenzied career. It follows the man like his shadow.

The great characteristic of the modern man is the fact that he forgets "the dimensions of humanity," as Ramuz has observed. Long ago the fabulist told us the story of the frog who puffs himself up and bursts. The modern man too wants to be as large as the ox ; he may even succeed, but he too will burst. Do not let us forget that our nature and our possibilities are limited. We can endure only a certain weight of sensations, just as our stomachs can tolerate only a certain amount of food. Accordingly, when we multiply beyond all prudence the number of our sensations, we must, if we are to endure them, see that each of them is lighter. The actualities of the cinema enable us to traverse the five continents in twenty minutes. But this is possible only on condition that our view of each item is superficial. Each sensation will have been deprived of much of its substance ; reduced to a mere pellicle, it will have little weight and will make but little impression on us. And so we are reminded of Alain's observation : "What is spent on speed is wasted."

And if it happens that we have to abandon speed—for example, if we have to give up the motor-car and to walk—we are struck by the fact that our sensations, less numerous, have in compensation become denser, more real, more rich in content, and we are not sure that we have not after all gained by the change. They have lost something in quantity, but they have acquired another dimension. They are not flung at us like so much confetti, but we hold them more firmly. "A bird in the hand is worth two in the bush." And are not the sensations multiplied by speed perpetually "in the bush" ? They will or might be ours, but do we ever hold them fast ? This chimes with what we observed one day in respect of the secluded lives of the inmates of the convent or the hospital; those lives, to all seeming, without happenings, but in which the most trivial incident assumes the importance of an event, like a trifling sound in the silence. There was a void to be filled ; here an overplus has to be rarefied. But the law is the same. No doubt we have always at our disposal a fairly constant sum of interest ; it distributes itself over more or less numerous objects, but is not thereby lessened or increased. Nature always obtains her due. (So, they say, does the devil.)

V

We generally admire, in our text books, our technical treatises, and in all letterpress whose object is to instruct and inform, a more open and pleasing typography than of old. One might almost say that wide avenues have been laid down through the text, as they are driven straight through the entanglement of ancient slums. Much has been sacrificed to appearances. Thanks to numerous paragraphs, to sub-titles in heavier type, the book has gained in clarity, at least to the eye. One sees which way it is travelling, and the reader sees where he is going, as when he stands at the entrance of a wide, straight thoroughfare. And we need not speak of the excellent illustrations. We admire such books, and there is certainly much to be admired ; yet one should possibly retain a trace of scepticism as to the didactic value of these admirable working tools. The truth is, and it is a curious fact, that the youthful minds which are shaped with the aid of these tools are much more ignorant than their elders. And having regard to the distinctness of these handsome examples of the printer's art, the mental untidiness which we remark is to say the least of it surprizing.

Yet is it so very surprizing ? Bergson made a profound observation when he spoke of the two kinds of order. Papers arranged in order on the writer's desk by his housekeeper are in order as regards the eye ; but the mind often finds its way among them far less readily than through the live confusion of an hour ago, which bore the marks of labour, and was its authentic order. The order of the intellect has subtle and complicated divagations. The old books, with their grey, compact text, forced the mind to follow everything, and to travel by the natural thoroughfares of the spirit. We may ask ourselves whether our decorative sub-titles do not set things in order as the housekeeper tidied her employer's papers.

What is clear to the eye is not necessarily clear to the mind. Just as one has not explored an ancient city when one has traversed its modern boulevards, so one does not know a book when one has glanced at its clear sub-titles and its photographic illustrations. Now, the danger of these tricks of presentation is the risk that they will simply catch the eye instead of inciting it to penetrate farther. They are too satisfying.

Undeniably, we understand how to simplify, and—to use the phrase again—to cut our way through. But we ought to realize that we lose as much as we gain, in subtlety and acuteness. We ought to realize that there are things which call for discerning and respectful attention, and which can neither be simplified nor cut through, or they die of it. And they are the most precious things.

VI

It is all very well, moreover, to cut our way through traditions. Traditions, whether they relate to dress, or customs, or morals, are complicated things, as confused as the ancient portions of our cities. The mediaeval survivals that people the British institutions, overlapping and interlocking in a thousand ways, afford

THE CLEAN SWEEP

a very fair example. For the most part they cannot justify themselves, but can do no more than take shelter behind their venerable antiquity. It is only too easy for the rationalistic mind to denounce the illogicality, and even the absurdity, of these survivals, attempting to drive through their jungles the straight highways which are more to its taste. Thus, for example, did the French Revolution; and this bold geometry is assuredly not without its grandeur.

In our own times the offensive against tradition has pushed forward in all directions with a fine, ingenuous energy. Modern youth would feel that it was failing in its duty if it did not despise all that has preceded it. As we discard, ever more and more boldly, portions of the costume of civilized people—or, to be exact, of civilized women—that used to seem essential, so we proceed to overturn whole categories of opinions and conceptions. Yet, sooner or later, the moment comes when we see, in some accidental fashion, that tradition had its merits. Are we to throw all our bonnets over all our windmills? That is soon said, and quickly done, but some bonnets have their uses, as we learn to our cost. For a long while modern armies went into battle without helmets; the helmet was obsolete, and no one suspected that its value was a mediaeval superstition; but then, of a sudden, it was decided that it was really very necessary, and it reappeared everywhere. More recently the straw hat was discarded; after a few severe and fatal sunstrokes it was worn again, and it may be that the day is not far distant when we shall discover that it was very imprudent of us to disdain the cotton nightcap.

It is true that traditions are the resultant of the play of conflicting empiricisms that fit themselves together as best they can. But we have only to reflect that the living organism was formed in very much the same way—by the action—how many times millennial! —of those encounters of forces which are summed up in the somewhat neutral expression, *adaptation*. This is why it is so bizarre, so devoid of apparent logic; why this long fantastically-coiled intestine, this unsymmetrical heart, this constricted liver?

It is really rather like the British institutions ; but it is in this way that Nature shows her wisdom, and it would be extremely rash of us to attempt—without serious and exceptional excuse—to replace these preposterous organs by straight, well-polished metal tubes. Let the prudence of the surgeon—that audacious man !— teach us to refrain from cutting, save with equal circumspection, into the jumble of human traditions!

VII

There was once a lovely little city, richly endowed with tortuous lanes and alleys, and with relics of the Middle Ages. It was famed especially for its fountains, which rose at each of its crossroads, topped with sentinel halberdiers, or adorned with colourful allegories, and equipped with radiating, sculptured nozzles that dispensed toward all points of the compass the boon of waters cold from their mountain springs. Like all remarkable places, the little city was discovered by tourists. They came to see it. At first the railway and then the motor-cars brought to it, season after season, day after day, its meed of ill-assorted, staring, cacophonous visitors. Then services of motor-coaches were organized. Who today persists in claiming that mechanical progress is contrary to the cult of beautiful things ? You can see very well that it serves the cult. Never had so many strangers come to admire the fountains—or to appear to do so.

The enterprize increased and prospered ; progress continued to do its part, so that longer, wider motor-coaches were built, more capacious and more profitable. Then it came about that these machines found it difficult to move through the narrow streets of the ancient city, and especially difficult to turn the corners at the crossroads, where the celebrated fountains with their nozzles certainly took up a great deal of room.

So they began to demolish the fountains. The motor-coaches continued to run as busily as ever, and the tourists were enchanted.

This true story may serve as apologue ; it illustrates to perfection the particular form of human stupidity which one might

call the modern folly. However, it was an ancient author—it was Juvenal—who wrote this line :
Et propter vitam vivendi perdere causas.
The Roman satirist was denouncing the unworthy patricians who sacrificed their honour in order to save their skins, and who thus, he said, in order to preserve life, cast away the reasons for living. An idea which has innumerable applications.

VIII

"Qui trop embrasse mal étreint." Grasp too much, and you hold but little. You cannot take everything. You cannot increase the load on one side without neglecting the other side. We begin to achieve wisdom when we have realized that the notion that we can always grasp a little more is a delusion. Our arms are still our arms.

"I am a man ; nothing human is alien to me." We too have extolled this motto. But it may be conceived in such a way that it becomes a snare. That is, when it inspires the desire to experience all states and all varieties of life. A novelist may do this, but it is a dangerous game. Many artists have burned their fingers at it ; such accidents, you may say, are occupational risks. But some of the greatest novelists have never felt the need of this sort of fuel. Balzac shuts himself up and re-invents everything, working from within. Ramuz, careful to exceed in no respect "the human stature," contents himself with his peasants of Vaud and Valais. He confines himself to them, but he grasps them firmly ; in them he finds a world, which is real, and has the ring of truth.

All the more, then, proceeding from the artist to the ordinary human being, the desire which we sometimes see him professing, not merely to "live his life," but to live all lives, is playing upon him a sort of confidence trick against which he should be warned. Here again we have the demoniacal thirst for sensations multiplied to the point of confusion, and we know well enough that it is anything but profitable. One may want to understand the criminal underworld, and to live in it in order to understand it ;

another thinks his education would be incomplete unless he had indulged in all sorts of drugs, and sexual aberrations, and various "artificial paradises". Will he be the richer for his experiences ?

It should be realized that in gaining experience of certain states one deprives oneself of the experience of their contraries. To scorch one's palate with all the more pungent spices is an experience, but it decreases the sensitiveness of the mucous membranes to a thousand delicate flavours. It is evident that the experience of family life, faithfully acquired as every experience should be, is incompatible with the experience of the life of a Don Juan. An acquaintance with the abysmal depth of evil concealed in human nature is of course an experience, but it is assuredly incompatible with a certain Franciscan candour which offers another and possibly more extensive experience. One has to choose one's experiences; one cannot have them all. Even if we admit that "it takes all sorts to make a world," one cannot oneself play all parts. Even an actor cannot do that. This reflection teaches one to be more contented with one's lot, and instead of regretting the experiences which have been beyond one's reach, to appreciate all the better those which destiny has placed within it, and which are equally valuable. A man regrets that he has never gone round the world, but he can still make "the voyage round his chamber". We were speaking of novelists; perhaps the best lesson they have taught us is that the humblest and narrowest life is in itself a world, and one that opens upon all the depths of being.

IX

Perhaps there is no novelist who has taught us this lesson more completely and more illuminatingly than Flaubert; nor one who has at the same time illustrated more emphatically the truth of the proverb: "Grasp all, lose all." He has approached the subject from the face and the obverse; he has revealed it in all its absurdity; he has examined it from every aspect. Let us follow this clue through Flaubert's work.

First we will open *Bouvard et Pécuchet*. These two comic

worthies are supreme examples of those who have tried everything and achieved nothing. They have experimented with the range of human destinies, committing the initial mistake of believing that one can try out a destiny as one puts on an overcoat. They experiment with agriculture ; they take up archaeology ; they study chemistry, and go from that to sorcery. They remain, in the end, the simpletons they were in the beginning, reduced to impotence by the very range of possibilities.

But what of *St. Antoine*, in the *Tentation* : does he act otherwise, though he dwells on a higher level ? As for the temptation that assails the holy anchorite, is it not, rather than the allurement of this or that particular, the multiplicity of the contradictory doctrines that appeal to his intelligence, so that his mental confusion becomes that of humanity itself, contending with the Babel of pleasures and intellectual systems ?

Let us pass on to *Madame Bovary*. Here it will suffice to quote an observation of Alain's ; he does not like Flaubert, but whether he likes or dislikes him he sees clearly. "It seems to me," he says, "that Emma Bovary is a Pécuchet in petticoats, who makes love as the other takes up agriculture or phrenology" (V, 54). Let us say that Madame Bovary, in her desire for the romantic, is essentially the person who wants to be what she is not, what she was never meant to be. In this respect she is at one with our two worthies. And in this, too, she is *modern*.

Now, in contrast to all these blunders, let us take the central character in the short story, *Un coeur simple*. The poor sewing-woman, who bears—an ironical presage !—the old-fashioned name of Felicité, is the person who has only one destiny—her own —and who abides by it. She is, as a matter of fact, too simple to be as deplorably double-faced as Madame Bovary, or as miserably multifold as Bouvard and Pécuchet. Her life is most intense within her narrow and even painfully restricted circle of interests and affections. And if at moments she is ridiculous, at one terminal point of the human lot, as Bouvard and Pécuchet are at the other, this is because there is something ridiculous in any human destiny, and because Flaubert is not able to forget the fact. At all events this simple heart is never a desiccated heart. When there is no one else for her to love there is the parrot. And when the parrot is dead she continues to love its stuffed effigy ; she centres everything on this fetish, until she ends by confusing it with the Holy Ghost ; a magnificent symbol.

III
ANGELISM

I

"A GREAT, sincere soul does not know what it is ; of all things that of which it is least capable is to take its own measure." This sentence, which is Emerson's, bears the very imprint of its author. It has his tranquil and noble bearing ; a sort of natural pride that seems to have surmounted pride.

To take one's own measure : that, since the awakening of consciousness, has been the constant preoccupation of the young of the human species. The child wishes to be the tallest or strongest of his fellows, the one who can do most in this or that respect. He measures himself against the wall, against the doorpost, in the hope of surpassing the tally that marks the stature of his companion ; he cheats if need be, standing on tip-toe ; he lifts his head that he may not lose an inch of his height. Later on he transfers this anxiety to excel to all sorts of activities. And what do the nations do on the field of battle ? We say they "measure their strength". The desire to prevail is one of the great elementary motives of all human conduct. Some have thought that it was *the* supreme and essential motive ; and here we have Nietzsche's "will to power".

But as soon as we come to less material and less tangible values, measurement, size, ceases to be an indisputable reference. Bergson is even of the opinion that the things of the spirit are defined by the fact that they are not measurable. In their case there is neither wall nor tally ; hence everyone is free to believe himself superior to another in this or that respect. And so he is. At the same time, he is never quite sure that he is not deluding himself. Here we have the origin of the sense of inferiority, studied so diligently by Alfred Adler, a sense which is in truth the cankerworm of pride. For it is never found without pride, nor is pride ever without it. Man is never sure of himself, and this unsureness is a constant and lancinating anguish.

Could not one find salvation is discarding once for all this hankering to measure oneself ? The "great and sincere soul" of which Emerson speaks is the soul that has achieved this liberation. Being sincere, it admits, upon considering itself, that it does not know its own stature. It has ceased to measure itself against others. It is enough to measure itself against itself, and to derive, from this measurement, now a just humility, and now a justified pride.

II

Such is the true modesty of great men, of those who have leapt out of the infernal circle of insane pride and the sneaking sense of inferiority. Here one must recall that other proverb : "He who seeks to be an angel becomes a brute."

This, of course, may be understood in a bourgeois, commonplace sense, as the somewhat spineless advice to be contented rather than venturesome ; to refrain from hastily entering upon the temerarious paths of exceptional virtue, heroism, or sanctity. But the Church herself, who desires this sanctity, these extreme attempts, and teaches that the Kingdom of Heaven is taken by violence ; that it belongs to those capable of storming it ; even she warns the faithful against the sin of "angelism". "Who seeks to make himself an angel becomes a brute." Thus understood the proverb is no longer trivial.

To seek to be like an angel is again and always to presume to measure oneself, in the hope and even the conviction that one will surpass the human stature. There are men who all their lives are subject to the obsession of the record, physical or moral, and we have already seen that this is essentially a modern phenomenon. These men cannot endure to think of themselves except in the guise of the champion. They want to surpass all others, for example, by their astonishing asceticism ; or they cherish the ambition of developing "supranormal powers". They see themselves as supermen. Alas, one can only tell them, as the frog in the

ANGELISM

fable is told by his sister : "You are nowhere near it." The prudent warning : "Who seeks to be an angel," etc., if one addresses it to them, is not wrongly addressed. For analysis will soon reveal, behind all these extreme ambitions, a very secret but very keen sense of inferiority, which seeks to compensate itself as best it may. Fundamentally, these are individuals who harbour the most profound and painful doubt of themselves, and who need all this flourish of trumpets, all this boasting, in order to silence the excruciating doubt. This is why their ambition is secretly undermined. This is why "the Tarpeian rock is near the Capitol".

III

If these extreme ambitions are dangerous in the individual, they are still more perilous when they take possession of a collectivity, a church, a nation. It may be uplifting to believe that our group has a civilizing mission ; but go a step further, and we have fanaticism, the stake and the fire, and all the madness of the wars of religion. We may be sure that behind all these excesses, which end by turning against their authors, there is still, and always, this intimate sense of inferiority. The psychologist is well aware that the man who believes himself elect and sees himself above all others is the prey of this ulcerous infirmity, and harbours doubts of himself that verge upon despair. But what is true of individuals is true also of groups and peoples.

An entire civilization may lapse into the sin of angelism ; or, if one prefers it, may be attacked by the *folie des grandeurs*. This might well have been the case, if we consider the matter, with our modern Western civilization. Its ambition is unbridled ; but we see already that this frenzy of ambition is a form of suicide. For such an ambition to achieve a record, to surpass all others, is already, one may be sure, full of anguish and doubts of its own abilities. What wisdom there is in the recall to normality so well expressed by Ramuz in his title : "The stature of man !" Or must we again recall La Fontaine's fable ? Perhaps we understand better now why

the puny creature
Puffed itself out until it burst.

At heart, the frog who puffs himself out and tries to rival the ox never really believes that he has succeeded. That is why he is in such need of his sister's approbation, why he pesters her with questions: "Am I not as big yet? Am I not as big now? . . ." But his fantasy is never confirmed by the other, and the psychologist suspects that *this* is what shatters him.

IV

Francois de Miomandre[1] feels that he is called upon to speak in defence of love—poor love, flouted by people who profess to have more serious preoccupations. We have been—he says in effect—very near requiring modern youth to proclaim itself quite above this sentimental nonsense; and youth, thus solicited, goes one better. "Of course," writes Miomandre, "I do not claim that love is under all circumstances inoffensive. But, after all, putting the matter at its worst, a man who commits a folly for the sake of love will cause unhappiness to at most three or four persons, while if his programme is to establish Paradise on earth . . . The comparison is overwhelming."

On reading, at the same time, a book by Romain Rolland—his *Voyage intérieur*—in which the author of *Jean Christophe* reflects upon his past, I came upon the portrait which he has drawn of one of his Burgundian ancestors, who took out articles of citizenship in his province under the Revolution, but who was none the less of the race of Colas Breugnon; a solid, sensible fellow who did not lose his head over systems, and whose heart was in the right place. If he declared himself a citizen under the Terror he did not allow himself to be infected by the morbid contagion of fanaticism. If he happened to risk his head "it was to save an innocent suspect from the infuriated crowd and its summary judgments". And here, his great-grandson observes, in the most unexpected fashion, and without intending any wrong to the memory of his

[1] In an article published in the literary supplement of the *Journal de Genève*, 4th July, 1942.

ANGELISM

ancestor : "One of the best vaccines against the frenzy of public passions is private passion, passion in the true sense of the word, love. During the red years of the Revolution, Boniard the apostle was madly in love." (p. 90.)

It is well that the truths of the "gay science" should be recalled in an age which thinks itself very strong-minded when it shows only disdain for whatever it qualifies as sentimental, insisting on the greater importance of its "realistic" preoccupations. It is perhaps high time that our age should perceive that its realism, in which there is a good deal of systematism, has led it to commit acts of sheer folly—which were also sanguinary. It is well also to recall that virtue may be productive of many crimes, and that Robespierre is not the only example of the bloodthirsty ascetic. There is a certain kind of asceticism into whose composition a great deal of cruelty enters, and this cruelty is very ready to wreak itself upon others ; when it shows itself in its true likeness. He who seeks to become an angel becomes a brute. And the worst of it is that he is often a ferocious brute.

IV
POLITENESS

1

PEOPLE are fond of speaking of a crisis of politeness. But what, in our days, has not been described as passing through a crisis ? Besides, it is possible that the crisis is universal. But perhaps this universal crisis finds a good enough expression and summary in the crisis of politeness. For the rest, it is the same with politeness as with so many other things. One understands their value better when one has to go without them : a sentimental effect of nostalgia, an intellectual effect of recoil.

Alain has made some very pertinent observations concerning politeness. "One is sometimes astonished," he says, "that the barbarians should be so attached to the forms of ceremonious politeness ; but this by no means proves that they have no brutal impulses ; on the contrary. Armed peace is never maintained unless this dangerous power of expression is regulated in detail ; for even things that have no significance are threats and equivalent to insults; hence the politeness of the diplomat, which resembles that of the barbarian." (*Quatre-vingt-un chapitres* VII, 2.)

This passage occurs in the book *Des Cérémonies*. Of course, everyone knows that politeness easily becomes ceremonious. But Alain chooses to emphasize the fact that here we must understand the word "ceremony" in its full sense, which is the religious sense. The ceremonials of the court, etiquette, protocol, and lastly, mere politeness, are so many degrees of a ritual which is becoming obsolete, but whose sacred origin is perfectly recognizable. The rituals of politeness, regarded from outside, may seem futile and arbitrary. But they have an important function, which is to hold in check the passions, which are baneful to the life of society. "Politeness," we read, "varies from one society to another, as does language ; but calm and moderation are politeness in all countries."

Certain customs are ruled by a convention which is also a sort of politeness; it may be absurd, but only as the rules of a game may be absurd; and it has the merit of being a rule where disorder and pure violence would seek to prevail. "The custom of the duel," says Alain, "holds the middle point between the rules of politeness and the ceremonies. It is perhaps the most perfect example of that wisdom of usage which considers, not without reason, that it has done much to control the passions when it has regulated their effects." Wars, which never have more solid pretexts than duels, would be less dreaded if the rôle of second or negotiator were better understood. But here the seconds want to enter the lists also".

II

"Politeness or war." Yet the antithesis is not absolute; war has had its politeness. "Let the English gentlemen be the first to fire." But all that is over and done with; total warfare is war without manners.

Actually, all warfare deals rude blows at politeness, and this has to be patiently reconstructed afterwards, with many other things overthrown by resort to arms. It has been asserted that at the conclusion of the wars of the Fronde the seigneurs were no more than mud-bespattered, clodhopping troopers, and it took no less than the salons of *les Précieuses* to lick these bears into shape a little; in which one may even find the historical justification of the mannered affectations of these ladies, and the complicated itineraries of their *Carte du Tendre*. After the war of 1914 there prevailed for some years, even in Paris, a "caddishness" which was peculiarly conspicuous in that capital of politeness. One might have encountered, in the literary salons, a young poet, fresh from the provinces, who, half seriously and half in jest, spoke of founding a league for the restoration of the ancient French politeness; and this seemed so extraordinary that he was nicknamed "the Diplodocus".

III

There is politeness and politeness. What we mean by the term is obviously what one calls *la politesse du coeur*. It consists in making the gestures of benevolence and respect with all the real benevolence, all the true respect, of which we are capable. Of course, politeness is bound to make the gesture even when there is little feeling behind it, and even when there is none; and so its critics will accuse it of hypocrisy. It is not hypocritical, any more than Philinte was hypocritical; it is simply wise. It is acquainted with the great psychological law, which one would do well to ponder, that our gestures are easier to control than our feelings, our actions than our thoughts. But it is by making the gesture that one evokes the feeling, as though by an incantation, and Pascal knows what he is talking about when he advises the unbeliever to begin by dipping his fingers in holy water.

The advertisers of every cereal know very well what they are about when they get you to accept their favour; when they induce you to pin it on the game is already half won. The Crusades began with the wearing of the sign of the Cross!

Action, according to logic, follows thought; according to psychology, which is often the inverse of logic, action precedes thought and evokes it. So it is not a bad plan to begin deliberately with action. The pedagogue knows this also; he has to begin by teaching the child gestures and attitudes; the mind, little by little, will flow into them and take their shape. Are we to call this hypocrisy? It is simpler to recognize, without shying at the fact, that everything is learned from outside, and that the body persuades the mind. Politeness is to make the gestures of civilization. It is well to begin with the former if one wishes to obtain the latter.

IV

"Speech is silver, silence is golden," says one of our proverbs. There is an Arabian proverb that replies, in its dignified Oriental style: "The word that you retain is your slave; the word that you release is your master." And this maxim seems almost as though it were ready to come to life in a little tale from the Thousand and One Nights: Already we can see its characters gesticulating—the Emir and the serving-man... It tells us that everywhere, in all

POLITENESS

times, men have recognized and illustrated the value of silence. Above all, perhaps, they have realized its military value : let us say, its prudential value, its value as a ruse of war, or of commerce, as the Arab proverb allows us to divine. "You should turn your tongue seven times in your mouth," we say, in the same spirit. But this is a first step. "Prudentia" is one of the names of Wisdom. Let us say that wisdom is a purer prudence, a prudence preoccupied with our higher interests. And if silence is in the first place a weapon in the struggle for existence, if it is artful to refrain from betraying one's plans, if the wolf walks with the gait of a lamb, if the conquerors conceal their plans and win more by this feint than by brute violence, silence is also, on a higher level, the weapon of the sage, and the path of spiritual conquests.

We know that Pythagoras and his disciples valued it highly, and practised it in their community, so that Pythagoras was called "the Son of Silence"—which is the title of the fine study that Han Ryner has recently dedicated to him. The Christian communities, in a later age, in various fashions, according to the rule of each Order, followed the Pythagorean example. And when anyone seeks to obtain a little respect and recollection from the restless creatures that we are, he asks us for a minute's silence. We are so constituted that this is a great deal to ask of us.

We have become unaccustomed to silence. It should be observed that silence means not only a pause in speech, but the absence of noise. For noises are voices ; they all speak to us ; they pester us like flatterers or insults ; they are intensive chatterboxes, bores. We need them to be silent as well as ourselves. Of course, it rests with us, to a certain extent, to maintain an inner silence amidst the tumult of the world ; but this is not always easy. So we must do our very utmost to preserve some moments of true silence. For it is in the silence of words and of things that we begin to hear the voices of the spirit.

V

To preserve some minutes of silence : but that does not depend on us alone. The modern world is a noisy world. And we see that this problem, like all others, becomes a social problem also. Noise is one of the major evils of our recent industrial civilization. We are beginning to realize clearly the sins of the machine, no less than its benefits, which dazzled us at first. But it may be that we have not yet appreciated at its true value the damage wrought by noise. Machines are noisy ; they spread noise about the world, and this noise is perilous to our nerves, to our sensibility, to our spirits.

From what angle ought we to engage in battle ? Perhaps through the politeness whose beauty, now apparently obsolete, we still recall. Politeness consists, first of all, in refraining from inconveniencing or embarrassing others. To make a noise is impolite ; and to be shamelessly noisy is to be a boor. Now, it is human beings who are responsible for all these mechanical noises ; so that in this connection well-considered lessons in politeness, a serious re-education in politeness, might have the happiest results. For if one only exercised a little goodwill quite a number of machines would cease to be noisy. Goodwill on the part of those who control them, and those who invent and improve them. If one expended on the invention of silence a merest fraction of the ingenuity which is expended on making a din, the face of the globe might be transformed.

When radio was beginning to become general, quite a little campaign was necessary to make the owners of receiving sets understand that they had no right whatsoever to compel their neighbours to listen to what they chose to tune in. As a matter of fact, there are still people who have not realized the fact, of which it is opportune to remind them. Lessons in politeness always have to be repeated ; and with each new invention we have to begin again. But we must not grow weary of beginning again. For some time now the countryside, the last refuge of pure silence, has been invaded by free-wheel tractors and cultivators. At their present rate of multiplication the countryside will soon have become an infernal, uninhabitable factory. Foresight and defensive measures are essential. I am tired of insisting that devices capable of ensuring the silent running of these engines are perfectly possible ; but the necessity of making such adaptations is the last thing anyone considers. In the meantime, unmannerliness is spitting and bawling like a mob of drunken helots over the entire surface of the planet. Do people realize that this is a serious matter ?

There is a duty of silence. And there is, therefore, a right to silence. It must be defended. Revolutions have been fought for less essential rights.

VI

People ask me : Do you, then, want machinery to be abolished ? By no means. We accept this machinery as a fact which we do not dispute ; we only wish it would become silent. We are not considering the question of expediency : that is a matter for the economists.

Yet, after all, if we are urged to consider it, why should we not do so ? After all, it does concern us. And since the competent people, the experts in every domain, have shown themselves so ingenious in leading us to disaster, incompetent persons like ourselves have a perfect right to see if we cannot reply to a great many questions with our simple commonsense. We have the right, for example, to ask, seriously, whether it is a very urgent matter to mechanize the countryside ; whether doing so is not throwing a number of agricultural labourers out of work, to join their fellows from the factories and the cities. It is true that machines are useful servants. If they deprive some millions of men of work, they also, from the human point of view, make mouths to feed ; but these, from the economic point of view, are useless mouths. Now, it happens that machines are also very good at killing ; in war they perform miracles ; so that even if they create useless mouths they are most efficient at closing them for ever, stifling even their last cry. In this connection it is just as well that they are noisy ; so that they cover the human voice, and make a clean job of it. Thus the economic loop is looped, and all

THE MYTH OF MODERNITY

is in order again. In short, we see in what direction the machine is the triumph of the human spirit.

No; of course we do not insist on the death of the machine. But we are weak enough to deplore the death of human beings. And if it were necessary to choose between the death of the machine and the death of human beings we should choose, without fearing to appear old-fashioned, the death of the machine. (And perhaps, in one sense, it will be necessary to choose.) At all events our present misery will have taught us no longer to believe in mechanical progress. It is a lesson that has cost us dear, but it is a lesson. Human progress, if it exists, is in another direction. It has nothing in common with the machine. Henceforth we had better regard that as proven.

VII

An advertisement in a newspaper (can it be meant seriously?) tells us that "Polite technicians are required." *Polis* is the word. Perhaps the advertiser meant to say *poly* (from the Polytechnique). But it is a pleasing misprint.

We were astonished—perhaps it was rather naïve of us—that so much ingenuity should be exercised in making noises, and so little in inventing means of silence. But we were speaking, it will be recalled, of politeness. In order to be anxious to refrain from making a noise one must be polite; that was the theory. And here is the corollary; in order that the technicians shall take pains to invent machines which refrain from making a noise, the technicians must be polite. Politeness must be instilled into them in such a degree that they will not abandon their regard for politeness amidst the preoccupations of the inventor.

Now, it is perfectly certain that there is no direct and necessary relation between technical capacities and politeness, just as there is no common measure between the machine and human progress. And here one may go a step farther; when the technical constitution has been, as often happens in these times, the product of a too precocious specialization, one may conclude that it will go its way without paying much attention to the simple human make-up which is at the bottom of education and politeness. There was, we may observe, a time when these two terms, *education* and *politeness*, were understood as almost synonymous, and those who so understood them were not so wrong. Today we tend to confuse education with instruction, and there is where the trouble begins. And if in addition we place the accent on technical and specialized instruction, all solicitude for the human qualities is banished.

It is not without reason that the cultural studies in general, whose inspiration is literary, are known as "the humanities". I have always been struck by something which is doubtless more than accidental—namely, the exquisite politeness of those who have devoted themselves to the study of Greek. Here is food for thought. And while there is no question of making everyone a learned literary scholar, it is probable that we have paid far too little regard of late to the eminent value of the humanities as a preliminary condition of all culture.

In short : because it is the specialists who are building our world for us, we ask that we may have polite, urbane specialists, in order that they may build an urbane world for us. But in order that a specialist should be urbane there is no doubt that he must not be too exclusively a specialist. There is a kind of rudeness in all extravagant specialism. Let the technician know his trade ; but let him be, above all, as Pascal has it, *un honnête homme* ; that is, a well-bred human being.

V
TECHNIQUE VERSUS NATURE

I

Nature : a singular conception, which proceeds from the sensibility rather than the intellect ; and which it is very difficult to define exactly. It means the countryside ; and it means instinct ; it derives from the Latin *natura*, which derives from *natus*, born. It means the origin and the substance—*de natura rerum*—the primordial, the ocean of being from which we are gradually emerging.

II

The Greeks were more sensible of man than of Nature, for the Greek genius was fiercely eager to extricate man from her matrix, to make him clearly manifest. But the Greeks had Destiny—Ananke—who was Nature conceived as the formidable power, the dread Mother, under whose blows man must fall in the end.

III

Nature the friend, tenderly maternal : here is a conception peculiar to non-Hellenic ages and peoples, to the mystical, romantic, pantheistic man who aspires to be engulfed in the ocean of being.

IV

The modern man is once more less sensible of Nature ; but for other reasons than the Greek, and in another way ; he has less sense of measure, of *his* measure. The modern man does not profess to deny Destiny, but he confronts it with technique.

V

Man has never worshipped anything but power. He worshipped Nature so long as he felt crushed by her power. He ceased to adore her as soon as technique appeared to have subdued her. After that he respected only technique. This is apparent even in the games of the modern child.

VI

Must we then proclaim that Nature is dead—that "great Pan is dead?" Will the historians of human thought one day have to date this redoubtable event between 1900 and 1950? And will they have to recognize that it was not without relation to the two world wars, in which the monstrous triumphs of technique over humanity were seen? And of which we were not fully aware?

VII

It is a fact that Nature, in a few years, has lost much of her prestige. The beauty of natural spectacles was a function of their solitariness or their ruggedness. A few palaces on mountain-tops, a few good roads, a few lines of motor-coaches, and the spell was broken. In other words, it was enough to make certain retreats accessible; by that very fact their access was rendered almost futile. It was like seeking to possess a virgin: a contradiction in terms.

VIII

The feeling for Nature is a religious sentiment. When "God is dead," Nature will presently die. Now, modern man, by his technique, claims to usurp the divine attributes. The modern man is Prometheus. But Freud has a question to ask: "How is it that modern man is not happy in his resemblance to the divine?"[1] Perhaps after all Nature exists and will in the end avenge herself.

IX

The summit on which a comfortable vehicle discharges its load of tourists will hardly seem the authentic Sinai, or even *la Colline Inspirée*.[2]

[1] In *Das Unbehagen in der Kultur*, 1930.
[2] Cf. *La Colline Inspirée*, by Maurice Barrès.

X

The increasing use of rapid vehicles is partly responsible for the loss of the feeling for Nature among our contemporaries.

To begin with: these vehicles are instruments of man's recently acquired mastery over Nature, in which we saw but now one of the causes of her decline. But this is not the only reason.

When we go walking in the country we become incorporated in the substance of the earth; we live on familiar terms with plants and animals; we steep all our senses in Nature; we are aware of every lightest sound, every faintest odour, every contact. When we pass through the same stretch of country in a motor-car it is hardly more than a quickly-passing entertainment for the eyes, as though we were turning the pages of an illustrated periodical. We are able then to judge of the importance of the humblest senses in our enjoyment of the world, and we realize how our visual sense, that haughty parvenu, remains external and remote. Nature, seen from a travelling car, is no more than a decorative background, a scene which we shift at will. She is a country that we treat as a conquered territory, and in which we remain foreigners. She is a ravished woman, who avenges herself by refusing us all access to her inner life.

XI

This does not mean that speed has not introduced certain novel elements into aesthetics. Moreover, the motor-car, by preserving us from contact with our fellows, gives us a keener sense of the configuration of the soil and the main lines of its structure. Will the habit of rapid vehicular travel substitute a geographical and geological sense for the old, essentially *botanical* feeling for Nature? But then we should have a Nature without a soul; the Nature of forces; an inanimate *thing*.

XII

In proportion as we subdue a being we always come to regard it more as a thing, as *our* thing. So the master regards the slave, so the horse-coper his horses. And it is thus that the modern man regards Nature. At the same time he refuses to see Nature as a living entity; he closes his mind to "a feeling for Nature". Compensation, Emerson would say. The more we subdue a thing the less we enjoy it. And if we possess it more intimately under one aspect it escapes us the more surely under another. It is thus that the gods avenge themselves.

XIII

This is consistent with the decline, already noted, of the "botanical" sense. Nature is no longer a being or a family of beings; she becomes an object, a mere obstacle to be overcome. She appeals neither to men's minds nor to their hearts, but to their muscles. There are no more excursions; only records. One "does" a certain pass or summit; one "does" things, but what does one love?

XIV

Here is a parallel symptom: botany itself is not so highly regarded as of old. The modern "tourist" is not afraid of decorating himself with appendages, and there is nothing to be said against them except that they are as little varied as his imagination: the rucksack and the camera... But we see the amateur with the green specimen-case slung over his shoulder far less frequently than of old. Another parallel: we have noted that in scholastic programmes botany is relegated to the background, and the botanical excursion is abandoned; a fact as incredible as it is significant at a time when the need for concrete education is being discussed so vociferously. And science, suddenly ashamed of the dear old vocable "Natural History," or even the modern equivalent of "Natural Sciences," thinks it more serious and becoming to speak only of "biology".

XV

If "hypocrisy is the homage paid by vice to virtue," "tourism" is the homage which platitude pays to poetry. "Tourism" consists in wandering (or being conducted !), with gaping mouth and complacent expression, amidst the things which the great poets have consecrated as beautiful. Consider rather the spectacle of certain motor-coaches !

XVI

"Tourism" has spoilt everything that it extols. Fortunately it has hitherto reached only the romantic regions, the famous sites, where Nature reveals herself in her more immoderate aspects ; fortunately it has murdered only the sublime. We still have Nature in her simpler aspects ; the simple countryside, the village, the cornfield, the brook (where it has not been canalized—but that is another story, to which we shall return). We still have the places that are not catalogued because they are not exceptional ; the lovely old farmhouse which is not a historic monument ; we still have these things. But there are still the posters and the estate agents !

XVII

"Tourism" is nonsensical.

What a paradox, to believe that it is the bastard offspring of romanticism ! The sites, the picturesque views which it professes to admire, are those which were discovered by the Rousseaux and the Byrons. But it has taken such pains to degrade these spots, to vulgarize their picturesqueness, that its object is really non-existent ; as non-existent as the goal of the Englishman portrayed by the caricaturist, who in a dense fog is on his way to enjoy— that being the proper thing to do—a celebrated prospect. Modern tourism has everywhere spread the opaque and suffocating fog of its inexplicable stupidity. Here one may quote Edouard Schneider :[1] "These people whose mission seems to be to fill all parts of the earth with their fruitless excitement and their incurable incomprehension of what they see" ; and Georges Duhamel :[2] "The automobile has not conquered space ; it has destroyed it, ruined it."

[1] E. Schneider : *Le Petit Pauvre dans ses ermitages* ; 1927, p. 284.
[2] G. Duhamel : *Scènes de la vie future* ; 1930, p. 100.

TECHNIQUE VERSUS NATURE

XVIII

Not only does technique make Nature accessible, but it also, as we have seen, transforms her. Now, the power of transforming Nature, if it is in the hands of unqualified persons, will inevitably be the power of defacing her beauty. And this is a serious matter. It is the pendant of the danger, more clearly perceived and often denounced, of surrendering science to men of a low moral standard; they will only do harm with it. An ethical and aesthetic culture ought to precede any technical instruction. Technique is only a servant. Pushed to the front, it behaves like a coarse and clumsy parvenu. We have to find its master. But modern humanity is dazzled by technique; it can see nothing else. This is why it is spoiling everything.

XIX

Dr. Alexis Carrel's book, *Man the Unknown*, quickly achieved a remarkable success; assuredly not without cause. It has received much praise and much denigration. We will take a middle standpoint; we will not say that it merited "neither the excess of honour nor this indignity," but rather that it deserves all that has been said of it, for and against.

A great book; but let us admit that it is badly written. What is the defect of this irritating style? It can be defined in a few words: the author knows nothing of punctuation and construction; one would like to send him back to his Latin exercises. All his phrases are brief and fragmentary and are terminated by a full-stop: stop, stop, stop . . . juxtaposed, hardly co-ordinated, without relief and without perspective, so that the least and most casual detail is presented on the same plane as the principal idea of the paragraph, and one has to make a constant effort to keep things in their right places. The author seems to have no idea of the genius and the resources of the language in which he writes.

Dr. Carrel was actually a Frenchman, but his work kept him for the most part in America, and one may ask oneself whether this author, who writes so well about the problems of the human environment, is not himself the finest example of that secret contamination by the environment of which he complains so bitterly. Side by side with passages which are definitely those of a great thinker there are the naïvetés and puerilities of the average American. The sentence relating to the Scandinavians, who represent, it seems, the highest known civilization, and therefore demonstrate the incontestable superiority of the Nordics, provokes immediate and elementary objections ("what about the Greeks ?") which do not appear to have been foreseen. And another sentence, relating to proletarians—to the effect that if they are proletarians it is because they deserved to be, since their sorry fate is the result of natural selection—is unworthy of the pen that wrote it.

Who knows ?—perhaps these flaws were inevitable. Perhaps the author is inspired by an unconscious sense of the contamination of his own intelligence by the poisons of the Americanism which he inhales, and against which the whole of his work, in so far as it is positive, is a vigorous reaction ; direct, pertinent and often pathetic.

For the whole strength of the book lies in this reaction ; not in the data which the author has accumulated, which are informative but often superficial when they are outside the author's speciality. It is not in his endeavour to produce a "synthesis" of what we know of humanity, an effort which he does not continue until the end is reached (because a synthesis presupposes subordination— semi-colons and qualifying clauses !—without which it remains no more than a collection of data, a mosaic). No : the strength of the book lies in his arraignment of modern civilization (of which Americanism is merely a magnification) ; in the manner and the plan of his attack upon it.

XX

On reading Carrel one is reminded of Duhamel's *Scènes de la vie future*, in which the author makes the same accusations in his own fashion. But whereas in the case of this book it was always

TECHNIQUE VERSUS NATURE

permissible to object to the writer (and many have not failed to do so) that he was swayed by subjective and sentimental preferences, the scientist draws his arguments from the laboratory. Here, as a biologist, Carrel is on his own ground, on which he moves with sovereign ease. His argument is based on the notions of environment and adaptation. The fundamental idea is very simple : modern man, by his technique, has suddenly created a new environment in which to live ; his physical and psychical organism has not had time to adapt itself to this environment ; at certain points, perhaps, is fundamentally incapable of adapting itself, for even this process is subject to laws. But this extremely simple thesis is examined from every angle, is developed in all its corollaries ; indeed, the author makes the most of it ; at the first glance it seems a harmless theory, but actually it leads him far afield. For the unadapted organism loses the reflexes and reactions which enable it to maintain itself in its environment. "We have not distinguished between what is permissible and what is forbidden. We have infringed the natural laws. We have thus committed the supreme sin, the sin that is always punished . . . Life always gives the same reply to those who ask of it what is forbidden. It grows weaker, and the civilizations founder." There is a veritable moral and physical degeneration, the lamentable results of which we are beginning to see all around us : "One would say that no accommodation is possible to the incessant agitation, the intellectual dispersion, the alcoholism, the precocious sexual excesses, the noise, the contamination of the atmosphere, the adulteration of foodstuffs. If that is so it will be indispensable to modify our modes of life and our environment, even at the cost of a destructive revolution. After all, the aim of civilization is the progress, not of science and machinery, but of mankind."

Why this mortifying set-back ? Technique, which has modified the setting of our life, is an application of the physical sciences ; it ignores the physiological sciences, the sciences of mankind, which are only beginning to formulate their laws—laws less conspicuous, more variable, but no less ineluctable than those of

43

D

inert matter, laws for which one must have regard, or perish. Even when our modern techniques take account of hygiene, for example, they depend, in this connection, on a very elementary physiology, which is subject to revision.

When we have recognized that something must be done to supplement the "lack of exercise" of an atrophied existence, we have not asked ourselves whether the activities devised for this purpose were really the equivalents of natural activities; we have behaved as though with living creatures anything could be replaced by something, no matter what. Above all, this process is followed in respect of sport. "Saturday and Sunday golf does not make up for complete inaction during the rest of the week. In suppressing the muscular effort of daily life we have suppressed, without realizing the fact, the incessant exercise by which our visceral systems maintain the constancy of the internal milieu."

Thus, modern man has entered into a cul-de-sac, and his situation is tragic. What, then, is to be done? He can pull himself together and in certain respects he can make a right-about turn. "From his childhood, the individual must be liberated from the dogmas of industrial civilization and the principles at the foundation of modern society." What is needed is an attitude which is really revolutionary. "Today we ought to fight the principles of industrial civilization as relentlessly as the Encyclopaedists fought the *ancien régime.*" It is true that the programme which the author proposes in view of the conflict—the formation of social and educative collectivities, based on new principles—all remains highly schematic, and is not sufficiently defined by the striking comparison with the monastic orders. But even though Dr. Carrel has not prescribed the details of the new order, he has at least formulated a diagnosis, and the interest with which the public welcomed his book shows that he is on the right track. He has aroused a salutary uneasiness; he has called our attention to the fact that something is wrong; he is, in short, one of those useful kill-joys who cannot be wholly disregarded.

TECHNIQUE VERSUS NATURE

XXI

In summertime the city-dweller feels an imperious longing to steep himself again in Nature. He does not always know very clearly what he expects to find ; and he does not always proceed very intelligently. Perhaps he thinks he is merely "turning himself out to grass," and that this is a simple matter of hygiene, like "taking the waters". Nevertheless, his whole being is interested in the adventure, and in the course of the last hundred years our vacations have become a part of our way of life in proportion as our urban life has become more artificial. More recently we have seen the formation of a category of persons for whom the summer holidays are no longer sufficient ; they are supplemented by winter sports. And what are we to say of the increasing habit of the week-end at the seaside or elsewhere, and the camping holiday ? Here, obviously, is an attempt to establish equilibrium. Commonsense, agreeing in this with the eminent scientist, suggests that it would perhaps be wiser to give a larger place to Nature in our daily life, and that nothing can replace this lack ; which doubtless explains our eagerness. But, after all, our life being what it is, this eagerness, this hunger for Nature which seizes upon us periodically, is the mark of such health as remains to us, and we should by no means disparage it.

XXII

We should rather see in it a sign, a symptom, from which there is something to be learned. Paul Hazard,[1] writing as a historian, recently explained how the love of travel has developed since the 18th century, in some places a little earlier, in others a little later, but presently making the conquest of the whole Western world. Then there were the vehement appeals of Jean-Jacques Rousseau, urging a return to Nature. It was the poets who led the fashion :
Mais la nature est là qui t'invite et qui t'aime.
And all the literary manuals tell us that in those days a new sentiment was developed, "the feeling for Nature." This development, this invention, at a historical date so near our own period,

[1] Paul Hazard : *La Crise de la Conscience européenne de 1680 à 1715*. Boivin, Paris, 1935.

45

of a feeling which has always seemed to me so essential that I cannot even imagine myself without it, has always puzzled me. Should not so curious an assertion be accepted with precaution ? Is it really true that until the approach of the year A.D. 1800 man had never realized the existence around him of a world of Nature ? I am afraid that this assertion may be as naïve as the primitive belief derided by Péguy, according to which the world began in 1789.

XXIII

I know very well what has been said by way of explaining in what respects the modern feeling for Nature, as we have known it since the days of the Romantics, is a new sentiment. But I am not sure that people have clearly realized what was most original in this feeling. Perhaps this was hardly possible without a certain perspective of which we have hardly begun to be conscious. If we study this modern feeling for Nature in its first great herald— who was, indubitably, Rousseau—we shall see that in him it has all the characteristic symptoms of nostalgia, which are to some extent confounded with his incurable regret for the mother who died on bringing him into the world, and whose phantom he never, while he lived, ceased to seek, whether in Mme. de Warens, or in solitude and reverie. To speak more generally, Nature was for him what he always lacked ; the company with which he peopled his solitary dreams ; the "country of chimeras," of which he says, somewhere, that it is the only country worth inhabiting. If, on the other hand, this ardent declaration of the claims of Nature, depicted as a lost Paradise, suddenly awakened such echos in Rousseau's contemporaries, it was because in them also, the sons and daughters of the deliciously artificial society which haunted the rarefied atmosphere of salons and boudoirs, Nature was something of whose absence they were beginning to be acutely conscious.

This, perhaps, should put us on the right track. It has not been sufficiently noted that the development of romanticism was contemporaneous with the industrial revolution, and that there may well have been a correlation between these two phenomena. One of André Gide's characters—in *El Hadjou le faux prophète*—announces the paradox that "if there are prophets it is because they have lost their god". Or at least, we might say, because they are afraid of losing him. Everyone knows that those who are happy rarely speak of happiness, and those who speak of it often do so in order to invoke it by the magic of its name, which has power over the absent. Everyone knows that it is the oppressed peoples who sing of liberty, and that "the Republic was wonderful under the Empire". Language is a compensation. Now, it seems to me, not that romanticism precisely invented the feeling for Nature, but rather that it invented the habit of speaking of that feeling. Romanticism called upon Nature at the very time when the invasion of machinery, the birth of the giant factories, and the rise of industrial cities was beginning to imperil Nature. One may wonder whether this hymn was not a swan song.

Since then we have seen the peril that in those days was only in a state of incubation increasing and taking a more definite shape. And if romanticism had any failing in this respect, it was not so much the excess and the emphasis for which it has been reproached, as its attitude toward the new world ; it had not quite the courage of its convictions ; it stopped short and lost its way amidst the picturesque, the showy, and the decorative ; an attitude which ended, in many of the romantics, in becoming self-conscious and embarrassed.

XXIV

I find neither futile picturesqueness nor self-conscious embarrassment, nor romanticism, in the book which Robert Hainard has published under a title which is at once a question and a remonstrance : *Et la Nature ?*[1] Throughout the book he speaks to us directly, as man to man, in a fashion that compels us to reply, to state our position, to reflect on what we are doing. He sees Nature seriously threatened ; he is aware of the gravity of this

[1] Robert Hainard : *Et la Nature ?* Pub. Gérard de Buren, Geneva, 1943.

threat ; and he has the courage to say—speaking as a man assailed in all that he holds most dear and essential, yet without fanaticism, without injustice toward his adversary—that this adversary is modern man. And this he says in deliberate, well-considered, penetrating terms that move and convince us. An engraver and animal painter, he reveals himself here as a writer and thinker. But the artist, the writer, and—if you like—the philosopher, are notably one and the same man. Very conscious of his purpose, Hainard thinks, and chooses to think, in the terms of his craft, and this reminds us of recent references to "thinking with the hands".

This plastic thought is singularly concrete, pungent, and adhesive ; it is never slipshod ; it has no lacunae ; it leaves a constant impression of a solid and vital contact. We owe to it many fine pages, in which we follow the hunter of images, share his adventures, and feel our oneness with the warm and innumerable life of Nature.

Elsewhere, in a prose that acquires, quite naturally and effortlessly, the qualities of an engraving, as though the author had not exchanged the burin for the pen, we find a powerful evocation of the herons of the marshes. But suddenly the page strikes a pathetic note. It is as though the image on the screen flickered out and revived ; and we are made conscious of a drama to which we cannot remain indifferent.

"In an office, a man is sitting before a sheet of paper. What is this sheet of paper ? It is the marsh—and our man is cutting into it with long strokes of his drawing-pen. In an atmosphere of dust and Indian ink he is tracing, while he waits for the midday interval, plans which cut into the rich peat, fell the trees, and drain the mysterious depths in which great fish are gliding."

The juxtaposition of the two scenes, the contrast between this wonderful marsh, teeming with iridescent life, and this obtuse and murderous sheet of paper, brings us to the heart of the tragedy. Robert Hainard's admirably concrete philosophy, at the thought of this sheet of paper, experiences a profound, embracing revolt, infallible in its aim :

TECHNIQUE VERSUS NATURE

"The noble commonsense of the fisherman, the village artisan, the peasant who feels the seed and the soil and scans the heavens, and of many more exalted persons who are also good workmen in their own trades—of those who know that reality is worth more than words—is becoming increasingly rare in proportion as a man's work is more subdivided, more rationalized, and organized with a view to the accomplishment of a definite and restricted function."

XXV

The cause we are considering here is not merely the cause of external Nature, stupidly mutilated in the name of sterile abstractions; it is also the cause of the natural human being, of Nature within us, which is receiving much the same treatment. These two losses are correspondent; the one is the image of the other; and this is why we feel that we indeed are constantly concerned, and that we are defending ourselves, and the most precious part of our being, when we seem to be defending only external Nature.

"For it is necessary to realize the gravity of the problem. The harm done is great already, even though Nature is so vast that it seems puerile to worry about its diminution. It must be clearly recognized that unless there is some profound modification of the progress of civilization, the disappearance of Nature will inexorably continue . . .

"The actual protectors of Nature play, perhaps, as regards the majority of human beings, the function of advanced sentinels, scouts, antennae. They bewail the disappearance of the bears, of vast marshes, of Nature in her majesty. But one day, and perhaps, under certain circumstances, before very long, it will be the violet in the brake that will have disappeared, at least, as a spontaneous growth. The surrenders to which one consents in order to avoid facing a difficult problem are of little avail, since a moment will come when the exactions of progress will be intolerable to everyone. All the more reason to face it while there is still something to be saved."

THE MYTH OF MODERNITY

The heir, as he is fond of reminding us, of a race of cautious peasants and careful watchmakers, the engraver always harbours a justifiable suspicion, which his contemporaries would do well to adopt, of the many ideologies that seem so empty to the hand that weighs and tests them, but which have the terrible power of destroying life.

Nothing is more disastrous, in this respect, than a certain "economic idolatry," which takes but little account of real human beings, in comparison with those delusive abstractions known as contracts, turnovers, export balances, and the like, and all the rules of petty speculation, to which Nature and man are sacrificed without hesitation.

And what shall we say of those other idolatries—the idolatries of technique and progress ? Again and always abstractions, and singularly lacking in imagination ; for "it is always easy to obtain an immediate result if we take no account of the consequences".

The worst enemy of man, an enemy that the thoughtful man nourishes in his bosom, is schematism, the offspring of abstraction. If we follow the path of schematism we shall not encounter the human spirit. The human spirit has need of Nature, and is threatened by all that destroys Nature. The alarm was sounded by Rousseau and the romantics. The cry of warning is uttered again today, more consciously, and in a more urgent and austere tone, by a few far-seeing men, foremost among whom we must reckon Robert Hainard. May a word to the wise suffice !

VI

BAUDELAIRE AND THE MODERN MAN

I

THE present epoch has produced aesthetes of a certain type who are adequately characterized by a single peculiarity : they are never weary of praising Baudelaire, and they cannot sufficiently express their disdain for Hugo. The quality of this admiration for Baudelaire is suspect. It is by no means certain that one could rectify the judgment of these critics by confronting them with the vigorous pages which Baudelaire has devoted to Hugo,[1] in which he shows that Hugo was one of the greatest sources of his own genius.

II

If they would have it that poetry begins with Baudelaire, what have they found in him that is incommensurable with all the past? I am ready to look for a reply in certain pages of Baudelaire's which are neither among the best known nor among the most conspicuous ; those which have undertaken to sound the praise of *maquillage*.[2] These pages will enable us to understand both the *Poèmes lesbiens* and the *Paradis artificiels*. They take us to the heart of the matter. Yes, the deliberate eulogy of the artificial, the unnatural, the declaration of war upon that Nature which romanticism had regarded as kindly, but with which it had finally nauseated the more fastidious ; and then an inverted romanticism, an anti-Rousseau romanticism, a Black Mass of romanticism; that is what is incontestably new in Baudelaire, incontestably *modern*. But is it the best Baudelaire ?

[1] In *Reflexions sur quelques-uns de mes contemporains*.
[2] In the essay on Constantin Guys, *Le peintre de la vie moderne*.

III

Baudelaire's attitude to Nature is defined by his commentary on Eugène Delacroix' saying : that "Nature is a dictionary."[1] The artist, according to Baudelaire, takes his raw materials from Nature, as an architect—for example—takes his from the quarry ; but he does not consider that Nature already has a structure, nor that she is worth representing for her own sake, nor that she has a soul which the artist must divine (for the "forest of symbols" which she offers us serves us to express ourselves only, and not Nature ; she is always "the dictionary"). In which Baudelaire is absolutely opposed to the classical Goethe, in whom the artist is the flowering of the naturalist, and who, as a good geologist, recognizes, in the very structure and strata of the quarry, the hand of the great Architect. And here he is opposed also to romanticism (though Vigny may perhaps be excepted). And in this respect he is indubitably an innovator.

IV

From this point of view one will attach more importance to the strange fits of wrath against Nature which often seized upon Baudelaire, and in which one might be tempted to see mere whimsical sallies. But his anger was something far more profound. "To those doctrinaires who are so satisfied with Nature, an imaginative man would assuredly have the right to reply : I find it useless and wearisome to represent that which exists, because nothing that exists satisfies me. Nature is ugly, and I prefer the monsters of my imagination to positive triviality."[2] An irreconcilable attitude, antithetical to life.

V

It has been said that Baudelaire, in departing from Nature, inaugurated the poetry of "modernity" and "the capitals". He was certainly keenly aware of these. But so was Hugo before

[1] In *L'OEuvre et la vie d'Eugène Delacroix*.
[2] *Salon de* 1859.

him. Here, as elsewhere, one may repeat what Denis Saurat has demonstrated : that almost everything that is in Baudelaire was already in Hugo (less visible because dispersed and, as it were, diluted by the thousand other aspects of a vast body of work). What is now in Baudelaire is not so much the fact that he discovered modernity, as the fact that he broke away from Nature, feeling that what was modern was anti-natural, a sort of "transmutation of values".

VI

As for Baudelaire's "Satanism," is it not simply this : the rejection of Nature in favour of his "monsters" ? For this was his supreme rebellion. The greatness of Satanism—akin to the greatness of Prometheus—is its will to create another world, to date the world from today. But what in Nietzsche becomes an anxiously joyful affirmation miscarried in Baudelaire, and was only half accomplished. He did not speak of the "creation of values," nor of "the superman". He spoke of "the artificial" and "the dandy". The misery of Satanism is that it achieves, in exchange for the lost Paradise, only the "artificial Paradises" ; and it is not deluded by them.

VII

What is novel in Baudelaire is full of risk and menace. He himself said : "Hell or heaven, what does it matter ! ... To find something new !" What he found was perhaps not hell. It was at least "the anti-natural," because he had not sufficient faith in Nature ; he believed her to be exhausted ; he saw her wizened, like his *Petites Vieilles*. "To the eyes of memory how small the world is !"

VIII

But while opposing Rousseau he was still closely akin to him. For Rousseau, Nature and morality are one. Now, we can conceive a criticism of romanticism which would be based on the negation of this postulate ; we can imagine that some people—

they might be realists or cynics—reject morality in the name of Nature, while others—and these would be Puritans—deny Nature in the name of morality. One point is well worthy of remark : for Baudelaire the two things are still united. He does not think it possible to shake off the yoke of the one without repudiating the other. And this is Baudelaire's tragedy ; for now only one path remains open to him : "the artificial," which for him is identical with the perverse ; he is in an *impasse*.

IX

The very notion of perversity proceeds from the belief in the goodness of Nature, since it defines the anti-natural and believes it to be immoral. Suppress the dogma of the goodness of Nature, and there is no longer such a thing as "perversion". And there is no longer any place for the Baudelarian attitude, which is really— as we see clearly from this angle—the negative of romanticism.

X

Our epoch, which has killed Nature, which has created modernity and the machine, which likes painted faces, and has invented surrealism, is unwilling to admit that Baudelaire's genius went beyond his denial of Nature in favour of "artificial Paradises". It regards him as its precursor and its justification. It is because it sees him from this angle that it so rashly contrasts him with Hugo. But in so doing it makes it impossible for itself to probe him more deeply, and to understand him for his own sake.

XI

But have not some of us begun to come to our senses, and to restore things to their *natural* place ? I have cited Saurat's opinion. Here is a passage from Guéhenno. In speaking of Hugo, he says : "We have seen great and authentic writers—one can only suppose that they are asthmatic and cannot breathe in the open air—profess disgust at this vast body of work. The criticism that does not entirely like anything unless it feels that it gains the upper hand over it by explaining it, has attempted to contrast Baudelaire with Hugo, the disciple with the master. It has been considered good form to despise Hugo as a facile, profuse and vulgar poet. I know no better symptom of the breathlessness, the enervation, the fatigue of this epoch."[1]

XII

The authentic, concentrated, glittering genius of Baudelaire is not where the critics have placed it. It is not to be found in the impasse into which he has plunged, but in the suffering that has driven him into that impasse, in the "aptitude for suffering common to all artists, and all the greater in proportion to their instinct for the just and the beautiful".[2] We see Baudelaire's greatness too in his astonishing appreciation of the greatness of others, irrespective of the Muse which they served; of Hugo, in particular, or of Delacroix, or of Richard Wagner, which he detected immediately. We see it in the complete artistic personality—so rare a phenomenon—which was able to perceive the "correspondences" of colour, perfume, sound, and ideas, and so to penetrate the essence of the Symbol. The greatness of Baudelaire is not to be found in the grimace which he imposed upon himself in order to obtain forgiveness for his greatness, and which is all that the more bigoted Baudelairians are able to perceive. He was great, not so much because he announced the modern world as because he foresaw it sufficiently to be tortured by it. We do not find anything of his greatness in the "maquillage" which he eulogised, but in the bitterness that impelled him to paint the complexion of a dandy or a pervert on the demigod that he harboured within him.

[1] Jean Guéhenno : *Jeunesse de la France*, Grasset, 1936, p. 193.
[2] *Richard Wagner et Tannhäuser à Paris*.

VII

OF THE PRESTIGE OF ACTION

I

To praise action is well enough. But only too often this praise implies a contempt for thought. Sometimes this contempt is not implied, but naïvely expressed.

II

Today there is actually a "mysticism" of action. That is, men do not require that action shall produce its credentials; they take it on faith; and the mere word, "action," is enough to excite and uplift them, as at other times the words "God, country, revolution" have done.

III

One may say of the prestige of action what we said of the prestige of speed. It is a bastard consequence of the myth of Progress: action is that which brings about a change in the world, and under the hypothesis of progress all change is desirable, since all things are proceeding from good to better. The belief in progress is abandoned, wherefore men cling all the more desperately, in defiance of all logic, to belief in action. One must have faith—in something.

IV

The classic age, which posited the supremacy of reason, was the reign of French culture; the romantic age, which exalted feeling, energy, and music, corresponded more especially to certain Germanic aspirations; the modern age is Anglo-Saxon in tonality. The prestige which it accords to action is integral with the prestige of muscle, sport, and performance.

THE PRESTIGE OF ACTION

V

Far from us be it, in the name of culture, to disdain feelings, or even muscle. Was not Greece, which in our eyes remains the supreme image of a culture, both Dionysiac and athletic ? But she knew how to subordinate everything under the supremacy of the *logos*. What is wrong is that one of the subordinate elements of this hierarchy should break away under the inspiration of a mysticism and exhalt itself *"über alles."*

VI

Enough has been said—perhaps too much—of the dangers, the romanticism, the mysticism of sentiment. A mysticism of action is still more dangerous, because action acts, because it changes something in the world, and because, if it does this without reason, it hurls us into the most desperate adventures.

VII

Art for art's sake is perhaps decadence ; but action for action's sake is savagery.

VIII

Those who keep on calling for "action, action," will presently call for violence.

IX

There is a relation, in the modern world, between the prestige of action and the prestige of youth. But a young man always runs the risk of being thrust aside by a younger, and an action by a deed of violence. Here is the slope of inflation and rising prices, peculiar to the modern mentality, which we have already denounced.

X

The mysticism of action holds liberty cheap ; and here it is perfectly consistent. True liberty is primarily liberty of thought ; it is not possible save under the supremacy of thought. But when action alone is supreme the only liberty is liberty to surrender to impulses, and to the most violent impulses. Then tyranny intervenes as the only principle of order. It assumes the function of delimiting the field of action—a function which, in better times, was precisely that of thought.

XI

Rather than "tyranny," the modern world prefers the euphemism "dictatorship" (supreme homage of vice to virtue). But let us call a spade a spade.

XII

One may wonder whether tyranny detests thought because it is free or liberty because it thinks.

XIII

Those who are on fire to act despise thought because it "does" nothing. It is better to act, they say ; even at random : merely to act. They forget that it is precisely the privilege of thought to function as an essay, an action in effigy, a laboratory of life ; to feel its way and propose a thousand combinations, even the most audacious, before submitting one of them to the crucible of reality ; thought knows the cost of the explosives of action better than action itself ; and it knows the danger of action.

XIV

"Always words and more words," they say, "and not an act !" Perhaps the time is approaching when they will be "curst with the realization of their prayer" ; when, before the ruins that certain acts will have accumulated, they will lament : "If only these had been merely words !"[1]

XV

It is better to think badly rather than not to think at all. It is better not to act at all rather than to act badly.

[1] These words were spoken during negotiations at Oran, in 1937.

THE PRESTIGE OF ACTION
XVI

Let us try to call things by their names ; there is no better recipe for sobriety. What is the true name of an epoch which posits the primacy of thought ? Is it not "civilization" ? And the name of an epoch which knows only action : is it not "barbarism"?

VIII

COMMUNIONS[1]

I

THE great collective exaltations are always astonishing to those who coldly regard them as a spectacle. Irrational and violent as passion, they are just as disconcerting. One does not know whether one should admire or execrate or pity them.

II

If possible, we will not execrate them, nor yet admire them, but seek to understand them. To do this we must think for a moment with the "historical sense". We shall then recognize, in these present exaltations, survivals as old as human societies. Here we see the Dionysiac orgy; there the totemic sacrifice. One must go back as far as this to understand the passions that inspire the crowd.

III

We must go back, above all, in order to understand the cruelty that broods in any exalted crowd, and which will break loose, with greater or less violence, according to the object of its exaltation. Cruelty mingled with adoration; ambivalence of the horde that slays the sacred animal. Among civilized peoples the sacred animal may be represented by many emblems; it is still clearly recognizable in the bullfight; but it may also be represented by the gladiator in the arena, or by the motor-cyclist who rubs shoulders with death on the speedway. What matters the drink, so long as it is intoxicating ? Manifest or latent, it is the presence of death that constitutes the background of the exaltations of the crowd. This is obvious in the exaltat ons of war, but we

---

[1] We have thought it expedient to summarize here some theses which will be resumed and developed in a work now in preparation on *Le symbole religieux*.

COMMUNIONS

need not take this extreme example. I witnessed the spectacle of the people of Paris doing homage to the body of the murdered President Doumer ; it was evident that on that day the Parisians were performing a millenary rite : they were devouring the totem.

IV

Remember what has just been said if you wish to understand something of the psychology of sport.

V

There are good people who cry : "Could not one at least diminish the risks of accidents on the speedway, and mitigate the ferocity of the pugilists ?" Who would not agree ? But perhaps this would be to deprive the exaltation of the crowd of its most substantial aliment. "Are not bullfights so much gratuitous cruelty ?" someone asks. They are. But beware lest the people who are deprived of them simply replace them by gladiatorial combats and human sacrifices. Such things have been done !

VI

One must be blinded by prejudice if one does not perceive that the communions sustained by religion are among the purest. To be sure, the experienced eye of the historian will detect, even in these, traces of primitive mentality, for the simple reason that they are there as they are everywhere, and the orthodox historian will himself recognize them without perturbation. The Christian eats the flesh and drinks the blood of the Lamb sacrificed. But here the primitive aspiration reappears only in a greatly sublimated form, which deserves at least to be respected.

VII

Of course, we should also respect the scruples of those honest minds that see only idolatry and bad taste in certain of the more authentically collective manifestations of religion, as in the collateral cults which the Church tolerates or encourages—the cults of Lourdes, Joan of Arc, St. Thérèse of Lisieux. It is true that these popular cults are not, on the whole, expressions of the purest spirituality. But our censors had better act with prudence ! These cults express a need of the crowd. Let them ask themselves, frankly, how they propose to satisfy that need.

VIII

A "religion for the people ?" No. Or at least, not, as one understands it ; as a toy and a diversion. Offer the best you have to satisfy the need of human communion. Offer something better than the crowded pilgrimages, if it is in your power. But beware lest you give the people, or lest it take, something far worse.

IX

It is like the problem of prohibition. It is not enough to prohibit alcohol. The question is whether the people will not insist upon getting drunk on inferior alcohols. As regards the intoxication of communion, the answer is obvious : people who no longer attend vespers or evensong go to football matches.

X

The modern mania for sport is intelligible only if we are willing to admit that it is a substitute for religion.

XI

We can follow the history of the substitutes which were offered to assuage the thirst for collective exaltation when religious feeling began to decline. First of all there was nationalism ; then the manifestations of sport. We have seen to what a sanguinary bacchanal the first led us ; and we are beginning to see to what a depth of inane brutality the second may sink. A society cannot instal the cult of idols with impunity.

COMMUNIONS

XII

Art offers a communion of a fairly exalted character. The typical art, in this connection, is the art of the Greek tragedy, whose Dionysiac and cultic origin is well understood. The tragic hero takes the place of the sacrificial animal. He is the "scapegoat". Evocative of "terror and pity," the tragedy is not so much the "catharsis" of the "passions" in general as the "catharsis" of collective exaltation. It has some of the characteristics of the games of the amphitheatre, and of the mystery of the Passion.

XIII

Thanks to "the films," we are able to define the myths of the public that welcomes them. Speed, the machine, dollars, and brute force, variously combined, obviously constitute the myth of the contemporary public.

XIV

Here, by myth, we understand a collective faith projected upon a few privileged symbols which provide it with the material of its cults and its "sacrifices".

XV

Thus, it does not seem wise to propose the communions of art purely and simply as the substitutes for a declining religion, with the notion that they would by definition be of a more elevated character than the games of the arena. The elevated character of art depends on the elevation of the "myth" on which it has built. The decline of religious sentiment in a given group ends in the formation of a new myth; it is on this myth that the art of the group will erect itself. If the myth is crude the art will be no more refined.

XVI

Of the myths of a people, of its exaltations and communions, one may really say what has been said of passion, romanticism, mysticism, and all things irrational. They are above and below the human level; and when they are not above it they are necessarily below it. One false step is enough. Let us ask ourselves sincerely whether our civilization has not taken this false step. And if it has, when it took it, and why.

IX

OPINION AND TOLERANCE

I

MONTESQUIEU warned us that it is better to seek approbation rather than applause. Nietzsche declares, more vigorously: "One is always praised or blamed, but not understood." Once again, does not Nietzsche the Antichrist appear as the unexpected commentator on one of the commandments of the New Testament : "Judge not" ?

We are only too ready to class people and things as good or bad. But is not this childish ? It is the young child who finds his bearings in the world of fairy-tales, and in the real world, by means of such categories. But in this respect, under many circumstances, we have remained absolutely puerile. We seem to think that people and things are for us a perpetual challenge to make up our minds about them. We seem to believe that our opinion on everything known to us—and on things of which we know nothing—is of vast importance, and that the world is always awaiting our oracular pronouncements. This belief leads to the politics of the saloon bar and the café—to the clash of prejudices, enthusiasms, and slanderous gossip.

We cannot hear an opinion pronounced without immediately supporting it or bristling up against it. We should probably do better to make sure that we understand it, to begin with, and to continue to understand it. Often enough that would suffice. Is it always necessary to agree or to contradict ? And this refers not only to private opinions, but also to doctrines and systems. Jean-Jacques Rousseau, the self-taught philosopher, devised a very sensible way of dealing with them. "I very soon perceived," he says in Book VI of his *Confessions*, "that all these authors were almost perpetually contradicting one another, and I conceived the chimerical project of reconciling them, which fatigued me greatly and wasted a deal of my time. I found this mentally confusing, and I got no further. Finally, abandoning this method, I adopted one which is infinitely better, and to which I attribute all the progress I may have made . . . On reading each author I made it a rule to adopt and follow all his ideas without mixing mine or anyone else's with them, and without ever quarrelling with him . . . This method, I know, is not without inconvenience, but it succeeded in its object, which was to teach me."

II

Did Rousseau recall the manner in which he had succeeded in teaching himself when he thought that he in his turn was capable of teaching others ? Read, in this connection, the *Profession de Foi du Vicaire Savoyard*, and you will discover a trait which has not been sufficiently remarked.

What seems to me the essential feature of his *Profession de Foi* is the manner in which he presents it : "I do not wish to argue with you, nor even to attempt to convince you ; it is enough to explain to you what I think in the simplicity of my heart. Consult your own during my discourse ; that is all I ask." It is in these terms that he begins ; and he returns to them in concluding : "My friend, never argue, for by argument one convinces neither oneself nor others." Here, as almost always, Rousseau shows himself to be a singularly far-sighted educator. Does he not give us the perfect formula of a religious education conceived outside the dogmas of orthodoxy ? To cut short every objection by affirming nothing. Do not impose your ideas, but allow no one to oppose them ; and to this end, simply propose them. The "profession" of faith becomes a "confession" ; I feel that this is so, I have aimed at this result ; as for you, see what you feel and to what conclusions you come. Here, already, is the entire formula of what in our days will become the formula of "religious experience". Not to engage in intellectual discussion, because the religious reality is not of the intellectual and discursive order.

OPINION AND TOLERANCE

It is only by a misunderstanding that it is regarded as such, or at least, is so regarded to begin with. Rousseau, in short, would have us begin by *collating individual experiences*. It is true that these experiences comprise arguments ; the Vicar reasons a great deal ; but one must note in what spirit he reasons. He does not think that these arguments are without lacunae, and that they must irresistibly convince the hearer ; he merely says : as for me, I reasoned as follows. His reasonings are the vehicle of his experience, or the topography of the track which his mind has followed. There are other paths, perhaps better. He is only giving his testimony.

III

Equipped with the clue that Rousseau has given us, let us return to the masters of philosophy : this Ariadne's thread will be an invaluable guide through their labyrinth.

Here, for example, is Descartes. As a rule, a modern reader does not find his *Méditations* very convincing. He finds them disconcerting. All that Descartes reasons about in these pages, in which he has by hypothesis suppressed the external world, is constantly referred to this world ; even when he speaks of a God who cannot be "a deceiver," for it is, after all, in the world that he has met with deceivers. All this seems arbitrary and unsatisfying.

In order to escape from this unsatisfactory position I would place as an epigraph at the beginning of the *Méditations* a passage from his *Discours de la Méthode* (Part I) : "Thus my intention is not to teach here the method that each must follow in order to reason correctly, but only to show how I have tried to reason. Those who undertake to give precepts must esteem themselves more competent than those to whom they impart them, and if these precepts are deficient in the least degree they are to blame for the deficiency. But as I am presenting this essay only as a history, or, if you prefer, a fable . . ., etc." Here already we have the position of the Savoyard Vicar, though it is less resolute and less naïve ; it is the narration of a personal experience. Now, while it is difficult to accept the *Méditations* of Descartes as demonstrations, we can easily accept them in this different spirit, regarding them less as demonstrations than as testimonies, understanding them as the narration of an experience translated into and disguised by the language of ratiocination. Seen from this angle the *Méditations* become a sort of *yoga*—as the Hindus would call it ; here is the history of a spiritual journey. Such phrases as this : "I will now close my eyes, I will stop my ears, I will avert all my senses," now make a very different impression. The whole work assumes a different bearing ; it has, as it were, a dramatic impetus that bears us along. It is thus that one should read the philosophers.

IV

I have read somewhere this criticism of an author : "One regrets that so vast an intellect, equipped with such exceptional erudition, should always display such diffidence in respect of other people's theories, and should consequently end in an often defenceless eclecticism." This criticism set me thinking. I am afraid that what is condemned as timidity and eclecticism is really the very thing that was praised, a couple of lines earlier, as a vast intellect and erudition. In effect, it is the misfortune of intelligence that it understands. But do we really consider it a misfortune ? Anyone who approaches the ideas of others with intelligence runs the risk of understanding them, and this would of course be a misfortune if he felt obliged to start a campaign against them. Understanding them, he will no longer be able to make war upon them, unless he brings to his attack upon them a passion which is alien to the regard for truth, and which is, to be frank, in bad faith. Pascal has told us that every idea is true from some angle ; the intelligent man, approaching another man's idea, will be able to find this angle, if only he has enough sympathy, or even enough prejudice, to bring to this operation the necessary good will. Then, if he undertakes to criticize another's idea, it will be in order not to demolish it, but to put it in its place among other points of view ; and this operation, if you like, may be called eclecticism.

But will it be timidity ? No more than it is timidity that makes the cartographer, when he is drawing the map of a new country, assemble the itineraries of the various explorers.

If today there is a general preference for an aggressive and negative criticism of other people's ideas, it is because of a belief that such criticism is the mark of personality. One clears the ground, one makes a clean sweep (here again !) in order to set up one's own idea in the place of the other. I am afraid it is only vanity that is at work here, not the love of truth, nor even intellectual courage. It is by reason of this vanity that we have so many theories about everything, among which simple mortals often find themselves at sea, unless indeed they take refuge in scepticism. With less vanity, less desire to shine, to distinguish oneself, we should doubtless have a better understanding of a great many things which are not so obscure as they are reputed to be. The truth is, not that human intelligence is so feeble, but that human vanity is so powerful. But what lurks behind this vanity is still and always a sense of inferiority ; we are so anxious to be original because we are only too keenly conscious that we have but little originality.

V

24th August, 1572 : St. Bartholomew's Day. What sinister images are evoked, as against the dark background of an engraving ! The feeble Charles IX appearing at night in the window of the Louvre, where the Colonnade was not yet built, while the tocsin of Saint-Germain-l'Auxerrois gave the signal for the massacre. When we learned of this from our school books, or later on, when we read the account, traced as with an etching-needle, by Mérimée in his *Chroniques de la règne de Charles IX*, it seemed to us one of those stories that belong to history, and which could no more return again than could the dead. It was a story of another world, which no longer existed, and one could not even imagine that it could exist. This perspective is somewhat treacherous ; it helps us to be less shocked by the spectacle. What we dismiss once for all to the past is no longer very real ; it is the same with things that happen in distant countries, among other races, to which we cannot imagine ourselves as belonging. In short, it is the Pharisee's perspective.

But this barbarism, this cruelty, were prompt enough to reascend the steps of time and burst upon us as the ruffians burst into the house of the noble Coligny. While we were complacently resting in our Pharisaic conviction of progress, our own age overwhelmed us with scenes of horror worthy of the days we so proudly relegated to history.

"There are no wars but wars of religion," said Alain in one of his *Propos* (V, 74); "There are no thoughts but religious thoughts; every man . . . persecutes if he cannot convert. Culture is a remedy against this, for it makes diversity adorable, but culture is rare."

Culture is rare; we have been too prone to forget this; and that it needs but little to sweep away the sediments patiently and carefully amassed. Then the old harsh soil reappears. The brute is there. It is not necessary to scrape very deeply into the soil. From lack of culture to intolerance is only a step; and intolerance is already barbarism. Culture must always be reconquered; we must not give way; we must always toil up the hill.

"Peace is the work of man," says Alain again; "and war is the work of no one. When peace is not at work, war appears immediately. It is like the false note of the pianist, the fall of the tight-rope dancer . . . Those who do not will peace with all their might will suffer war." (V, 71).

VI

He who is certain that he possesses the absolute truth cannot be tolerant.

VII

Is the progress of tolerance during the last few centuries a sign of increasing humanity? Is it not rather due to a decline of belief? It is enough to note what fanaticism our contemporaries betray when they are recaptured by some brutal and simple belief.

OPINION AND TOLERANCE

VIII

It must be admitted that the majority of tolerant persons are sceptics ; and in the face of the intellectual deliquescence which is signified by scepticism one can understand that vigorous natures may come to desire a return to fanaticism and the inquisition.

IX

"Is it not possible," one may ask, "to adhere firmly to a belief and to tolerate other opinions ?" But this will be to tolerate them as errors. And this, as a matter of fact, is the first meaning of the word tolerance, which has been bequeathed to us by the ages of fanaticism, and which signified only a forbearance that was full of disdain. But by tolerance we mean something more than this : we should like it to be respectful and benevolent. And then, this is the whole question : is this tolerance possible without scepticism ? Does this meekness presuppose this abdication of the intellect ?

X

Fortunately one can perceive another basis of tolerance. This is *relativism* : an intellectual attitude to which the most recent findings of science have accustomed us. Relativism must not be confused with scepticism. The latter denies all truth, the former superimposes many truths, each true upon one plane and in its place on a scale of magnitudes. It requires a certain agility in the rapid change of perspectives ; and this is a discipline which is not acquired in a moment ; but it is as salutary for the intelligence as it is beneficent for human relations.

XI

Allow relativism to extend from physics to psychology ; it then spontaneously becomes tolerance.

XII

A great step towards psychological relativism was made when the subconscious was discovered, and above all when it was realized that the ideas and beliefs of each of us are only the external façade of unconscious realities. These *translate* themselves, one might say, into the language of ideas and beliefs. But the subjacent realities bear much more similarity among themselves than do the idioms that express them.

XIII

Let us remember this formula as the golden key of tolerance : *The ideas and beliefs of each one of us are merely a language.* To ask if they are true or false is hardly more sensible than to ask if French is true and English false. All ideas, all beliefs express a certain human truth. All deserve to be given the most respectful hearing.

XIV

Better still, let us try to speak to each of our fellows in his own language. To adopt, by hypothesis, the ideas and beliefs of the person to whom we are speaking at the time of speaking is a difficult exercise, but not an impossible one. It is, for example, the attitude which the practising psychologist, the mental physician, is bound, willy nilly, to adopt ; for he necessarily adapts himself to the psychism of his patients (and in his eyes their opinions are only part of their psychism), as the bodily physician adapts his prescriptions to the temperament of his patients. Might not this attitude, tolerant by necessity, and, if you like, by a sort of professional distortion, be maintained, to a certain extent, outside the consulting-room ? May it not be an indication as to our own behaviour ?

XV

He who is certain that he possesses the absolute truth cannot—we said—be tolerant. Nor can he be a psychologist.

XVI

Of course, to anyone who is not accustomed to it, this attitude, which one may call psychological, and which amounts to speaking to anyone the language of his ideas and beliefs, will be disconcerting and even shocking. One may regard it, in the first place, as a mere diplomatic untruth. But if it is inspired by a genuine intellectual relativism, it is easy to see that it is anything but hypocritical ; it is no more hypocritical than the attitude of the physicist who utilizes now the ordinary geometry, and now the non-Euclidian constructions.

XVII

To commonsense an idea is "true" or "false" accordingly as it corresponds or does not correspond to an object as the portrait corresponds to the model. Philosophy made short work of this conception a long while ago (and pragmatism gave it the *coup de grâce*). But a point of view which is henceforth imposed upon us by psychology is that an *idea, a belief, derives its signification for the thinking subject only from the chains of conscious and unconscious associations of which it is the termination and the emergence.* Let us suppose, to take the most favourable case, that an idea could be proven to be "false" from the extrinsic standpoint (that is, inadequate to a corresponding object), and that we could convince of its falsity a person who had hitherto accorded this idea a great importance in his life. He is very liable to reject, with this idea, the whole network of associations which for him it carries with it, and this network, no doubt, contains vital internal truths. The new attitude to life of the person thus deprived will be far more erroneous than his former attitude. We shall have *deceived* him in a perilous manner. We should have been more *truthful* towards him if, we had adopted the language of his idea (at least, after first dissociating it from the intimate aggregation which it expresses for him : but this is not an easy thing ; it is a whole psycho-analysis). The result will be the more regrettable if the idea in question is one around which, in the subject's mind, essential values are crystallized.

XVIII

The positivistic teachers have committed, in respect of the average Western man, precisely the mistake we have just defined.

They have deprived him, along with the beliefs they regarded as false, the spiritual values which were for him, which had been for centuries, inextricably woven into the tissue of these beliefs, and which doubtless contained more "truth" than the beliefs (even from the positivist point of view) contained of "error." Here is a crude and lethal surgery, which, in attempting to operate on some tumour, tears out with it essential tissues. The positivist spirit, which at one time represented itself as the integral scientific spirit, was singularly deficient in psychology. Fortunately the science of psychology appeared shortly afterwards. And the *psychological spirit* is the very antidote which is capable of correcting and modifying the dogmatism implicit in the positivist spirit.

XIX

One may still ask oneself whether this principle, that "every belief is only a language," is not in actual fact a subterfuge, concealing a subtler form of scepticism; and it is true that the sceptics will accept it without difficulty. But will not those who really believe, and take their belief seriously, be wounded by it?

Let it suffice here to invoke the testimony of the mystics. According to them, is not the formulation of any belief essentially inadequate? Is it anything more than a crude translation of the "ineffable"? Thus the mystics—a remarkable fact—have adopted our position before us.

If, then, our principle is capable of rallying the mystics on the one side, and the sceptics on the other, the odds are all in our favour—it will surely afford us an acceptable position, not only as regards all the forms of belief, but also in respect of all degrees of belief.

XX

Apart from relativism, there is another very valuable basis of tolerance—and by this we always mean a respectful tolerance. This other basis is what we may call humanism. *The human first of all.* (This is the antithesis and antidote of the principle of "politics first" which has wrought such disasters in our day). It is to admit that the human being is worthy of unconditional respect. And that ideas and beliefs are the efflorescences and expressions of the human, before being, in a diverse but always relative and modest degree, what we may call the approach works investing reality.

XXI

To base tolerance on the human is to say, at the same time, where it ought to stop. Its limit is, precisely, the inhuman. The fanatical doctrines that build pyres and open torture-chambers, which not only are intolerant, but plume themselves on being so, have no longer any right to tolerance. They have placed themselves, from the human standpoint, outside the law. But Voltaire has already said this.

XXII

Relativism is the fruit of scientific discipline. As for humanism, as we have just defined it, it would soon become what the Renaissance meant by the word, and would base itself firmly on "the humanities". Does not this amount to saying that a wide and lofty culture is the most reliable guarantee of a true tolerance ? Tolerance is not taught, but it adds itself to culture "as to youth its bloom" ; and any regression of culture must involve a relapse into intolerance.

XXIII

As for the psychological spirit, a completely new attitude to which only a few minds have become accustomed : if it seems to hold a privileged position in this respect, it is because it represents relativism as applied to the human being. It is assuredly the essential basis of respectful tolerance ; since it has, for ideas and beliefs, the twofold respect of the humanist for the human being and of science for its object.

X

HUMANISM

I

THIS line of Latin verse is often quoted : *"Homo sum ; humani nihil a me alienum puto ;* I am a man ; I hold that nothing that is human is alien to me." But those who quote the words are not so often aware of their author. This is one of those quotations that live so fully with a life of their own that their origin is forgotten. If you ask a friend who has "taken the humanities" to tell you who wrote this line, he will perhaps reply, Seneca, or Lucretius, or Horace . . . As a matter of fact, it was the comic poet, Terence (and if one does not always think of Terence, it is perhaps because the words do not sound comical ; they rather incline the mind to gravity and reflection). They occur in the first scene of *His Own Executioner*. This is a dialogue between two neighbours ; the one, Chremes, reproaches the other, Menedemos, with wearing himself out by overwork ; he is too hard on himself. Menedemos politely tells him, in effect, to mind his own business. To which Chremes replies : "I am a man ; I hold that nothing that is human is alien to me."

But this speech has detached itself from its context and made its own way through the world. It deserved to do so. Is not the man worthy of the name one who takes note of his neighbour's way of life, and regards him as truly his neighbour, even if he is astonished or shocked by his behaviour ; and who, by the exercise of sympathy, tries to explain those manners, tastes, and opinions, which differ from his own ?

Conversation, travel, reading are so many means of training this sense of others, this sense of humanity. Certain sciences—history, ethnography—help to train it. Literature, which is a representation of human types, examined and re-examined and

HUMANISM

displayed before our eyes in a thousand ways, is the most precious auxiliary of all in this work of education. This is why the study of literature has been so finely named "the humanities".

This line of Terence appeals not only to the intellect, but also to the heart. It inculcates not only an act of cognisance, but also an act of benevolence, which is not unrelated to the vast "charity of the human kind" of which the Stoics have spoken. And while it is true that the word "humanities," in the plural, signifies *les belles-lettres*, does not the same word "humanity," in the singular, signify a virtue which is very close to this charity ? And there are cases in which the singular says more in this sense than the plural.

II

We must not forget, when we speak of humanism, that this conception is bound up with that of the Renaissance. On emerging from the Middle Ages the humanists regarded classical antiquity as the most substantial summation of human experience ; but they were less concerned with placing it in a museum than with using it to revivify the present and the future. There is no humanism without this double movement: we seek to steep ourselves in the richest traditions of culture, in order that the still living sap may swell the life to be.

III

Humanism is an equilibrium. On the one side is the builder, the leader, who makes a clean sweep of tradition in the name of action and technique ; on the other side is the man of letters, the mandarin, who takes infinite delight in the classic texts without bringing them to life. Both are equally remote from humanism. It is only too easy to fall into one or the other groove. That is why humanism is rare.

IV

When I try to recall, among the men I have met, those who seem to have been the best embodiments of a living humanism, a few figures occur to me immediately : Carl Spitteler, Rabindranath Tagore, Romain Rolland, Freud, to name only the dead... It is true that they were, above all, great minds. But what else ? The true humanists—despite M. Julien Benda—could not be *des clercs qui trahissent* ?

V

Humanism, in every period, must wear a different countenance, since its function at any moment is to turn the course of culture in the direction of men's vital needs. Is it not the task of a modern humanism to direct the mind toward the building up of a social group, above the approaching catastrophic anarchy of industrial and national egoisms, but at the same time to defend the human personality against the ever-threatening oppression of the group thus reinforced ?

VI

The obstacle to the flowering of a humanism at the present time is, in the sphere of culture, the overwhelming accumulation of heterogeneous riches, and in the sphere of action, the complex multiplicity and urgency of the tasks to be accomplished. In either sphere, how is a choice to be made ?

Here the psychological spirit seems to provide a principle of order and perspective, since it is situated at the juncture of the sciences and the "humanities",[1] and concerns itself with the profoundest of human needs. Should not this be the starting-point for the builders of the required "new humanism" ?

VII

There is a charming Arab tale, of which we find a variant in Anatole France, and another in Maurice Kuès :

A certain Sultan sent word to the sages and dervishes of his country, to the effect that they were to provide him with wisdom. These learned men set out in search of it, collecting, throughout the country, the books whose contents they considered most

[1] In the last chapter of *L'Ame et l'action* (Ch. Baudoin, pub. Collection Action et Pensée, Editions du Mont-Blanc.)

HUMANISM

valuable. At last a long caravan presented itself before the Sultan. There were the sages, followed by a whole file of camels, each of which was laden with as many books as it could carry. The Sultan was at that moment engaged in some festivity, so that he did not feel inclined for study. "This is too much," he said ; "I could not read all that ; if I read it with my own eyes, how could I incorporate it in my life ? No, no ! It is for you, wise men, to extract for me, from all this farrago, a judicious selection of the best books, the only essential ones." The sages set to work again ; they read and re-read the books, they argued and calculated, discarding this, retaining that. At last a small party of sages, chosen from among the most illustrious, presented themselves before the Sultan with a single camel, which was laden with books. The Sultan was then smoking his nargileh, which inclined him to indolence. "Your college has accomplished an admirable task," he said. "But there are still far too many books. This camel can hardly bear them ; how then should I carry them ? Continue your excellent work. It is your business, and not mine, to read the books. Read these excellent books again, and make a choice ; draw from them an elixir of knowledge and wisdom. Compound it yourselves in a book more excellent than all these excellent books, so that it will be enough for me to read this single book in order to possess all that the wisest men of all the centuries have observed, deduced, and thought." Some further months went by, during which the wise men laboured and did their utmost to extract the quintessence of wisdom. At last the Grand Dervish appeared alone before the Sultan, with a single book, bound in the finest Cordova leather. The Sultan was then on his way to his harem. "That is very good," he said, "but it is too much ; continue without respite, and from all this extract for me a single phrase which contains all that it is needful to know, as the grain of incense contains all the perfume and releases it when it is burnt in the censer." The Grand Dervish set to work, and was at last able to present to the Sultan this sentence, written with Indian ink on a sumptuous parchment : "Man is born feeble and naked. He increases in strength and desire. He obtains less by his strength than he covets by his desire; then he declines and dies." The Sultan was then setting out for the seat of war. "I know that," he said, wrathfully. "You are all rascals!"

From this one may draw several morals. The wisest is perhaps that which Alain expresses in one of his *Propos*: "Culture is not transmitted and cannot be summarized."

XI

ELOQUENCE ON TRIAL

I

Vir bonus, dicendi peritus

IN our days eloquence has, as they say, "a bad press". But may it not be that the press is to some extent killing eloquence ? And can humanity be quite certain that it will profit by the exchange ? If the art of oratory has its recipes for seducing reason and insidiously evoking conviction, the press can hold its own at this game ; and as long as men read the newspapers they will be very ill-advised to lodge such a complaint against eloquence. Moreover, I do not know that men have ever complained of being led and deceived, and the accusation which the modern man has brought against eloquence has actually a different bearing.

Our contemporaries, if we understand them rightly, want no more "phrases" ; they want "facts". They treat the orators with compassion ; they esteem only the "technicians". To the "word" they oppose the "thing" ; in this they think themselves very wise, and "wink the eye" like the "last men" foretold by Zarathustra. In choosing the thing as against the word they do not realize that they are boldly engaging in one of the most arduous of debates, in which the great minds of other ages were passionately opposed ; they do not know that they are upholding the "nominalism" of Roscelin and Occam against the "realism" of St. Anselm and Guillaume de Champeaux ; but all this is philosophy, and our moderns, who know nothing of philosophy, nevertheless know that they ought to despise it.

II

These clever folk refuse to be "put off with words" ; or at least, so they think. They want facts, and more precisely, the sort of facts they call *positive* (though this is only a word ; but they do not realize it, and when they have pronounced it they feel rather pleased with themselves). They are positive people, who profess to be guided only by actual data, by reality "without phrases," as it might be presented by a photograph, a film, a number. And here we come to the sophistry on which these clever folk have based their conduct. They do not see that even the photograph, the film, the number, are always merely tokens, just as words are tokens : of whatever kind is arbitrary, in so far as the moments of reality which have entered into the texture of the token have been arbitrarily chosen from a multiplicity of others. This arbitrariness can be cancelled only by the intervention of a legitimate and tested principle of *choice*, of abstraction, and this principle can be provided only by *thought*. Moreover, even where this principle has intervened we shall not on that account grasp the fact ; we shall never obtain anything but a selective and subjective representation of the fact. But the principle itself is less and less frequently applied by the modern man. His methods of information, as they have been developed by the newspaper, the film, the loudspeaker—which one might call impressionistic— result increasingly in a series of instantaneous impressions, sparkling, leaping, electrical, epileptic, following one another without order and without connection. They are facts, no doubt ; facts, and again facts (or at least, what one has agreed to give the *name* of facts !). But who can fail to see—if he is still able to reflect— how deceptive this kaleidoscope is ? One recalls Valéry's profound comment on the cinema : "The false presented by the true." To believe that what we see is a view of reality is a naïveté of which only a "modern man" is capable. In short, although they repudiate the superstition of the word, our contemporaries accept without flinching the superstition of the fact, which is no less deceptive. The "fact" in which they place such confidence is a very precarious support, since it does not enable them to defend themselves effectively against the word ; since these circumspect people, these electors, vote for words, and as soldiers they die for words.

III

This superstition of the "fact", the "positive fact", is on the whole no more than a clumsy and pathetic attempt of barbarians to assimilate the scientific spirit; but the truth is that our positive thinkers are about as scientific as cannibals newly converted are Christian. The superstition of the fact is to science precisely what the ancient superstition of the word and the fine phrase is to the art of literature; for the debate that has developed in our time between the classic culture and "modern culture", between the "humanities" and the "sciences," is only one aspect of the examination which we have undertaken. We should be doing a great wrong to the humanities if we were to judge them by the superficial polish which certain rhetoricians have acquired by their contact with them—the very same wrong that we should be doing the sciences if we were to measure them by what the "positive" thinkers have made of them.

The truth is that in this debate between the "word" and the "fact" it is *thought* alone that is capable of organizing the facts and nourishing the words, so that the former are no longer momentary pinches of dust, nor the latter mere "puffs of wind". The function of thought is to assemble the facts which constitute experience and express their sap in order to nourish the word, for we must not forget the degree of solidarity that always exists between them; and in this way there will be a harmonious circulation of life between the three regions of the mind. The human problem is, not to choose between the fact and the word, any more than the problem of education is to choose between the sciences and *belles-lettres*. The only problem is to learn how to think. It is true that this is sometimes much more difficult.

IV

It is true also that the word is futile if it is not the plenitude of a thought which itself is rich in experience; but in its turn the fact is futile which is not organized by thought—the thought of which the word is the flowering and the inevitable form. In the present state of affairs the second truth should perhaps be more urgently upheld than the first. In other words, the educational significance of the "humanities" more than ever demands recognition. After all, when we encounter a great modern orator—who is almost an anachronism—we ought to hear him with close attention and great respect. I mean an authentic orator, a representative of the classic formula of eloquence : *vir bonus dicendi peritus* ; who would hold with Aristotle that rhetoric is above all philosophy ; refusing to divorce the form from the substance. This divorce is the doing of the rhetoricians of the decadence ; who imagined that the form can suffice in itself ; who were attacked by Quintilian ; who were responsible for the discredit which was to fall upon eloquence. Such discredit that today the very name of "oratory" has become a term of disparagement.

V

I can see yet another and a serious reason for the decline of the oratorical art in the modern epoch.

Eloquence is an eminently *social* accomplishment. This does not merely mean that it presupposes a public ; for that is obvious. But it presupposes, or creates, a *group*, coherent and complete, in the strictest psychological sense. *The oratorical act is a reproduction of the essential act by which all groups, and society itself, incorporate themselves.* In the shadows cast by the orator, and by the crowd controlled by his words, the sociologist and psychologist seems to be gesticulating, the magician who lays a spell on the primitive tribe and exercises over it the powers of guidance. Have we not here the original group, consisting essentially of the terrible and sacred Father, gathering about him the people of his sons, all equals, who communicate in mystical participation and identity?— The totemic group whose pattern Freud has rediscovered under the weft of any coherent crowd.

The act of oratory, which is an act of collective suggestion and communion, is the social act *par excellence*—the true "*contrat social*". This is why the Romans, who more than any nation spread throughout the peoples the sense of social cohesion and civic organization, were the great masters of the art of oratory ; why it is from them that we derive the name of tribune ; why their very genius, in all its manifestations, retains the lofty oratorical manner which constitutes its majesty ; and, in the eyes of the modern world, its vanity ; and lastly, why the Catholic Church and the French Revolution, which were the two most authentic nurslings of the Roman wolf, were no less fruitful of oratorical movements than apprehensive of *unity*.

Conversely, the decadence of the oratorical art is a necessary symptom of a disorganization of the social order. This may be verifying itself today. It is perhaps one reason why we should not be too ready to acclaim this decadence of speech as a sign of intellectual progress, as our lovers of "facts" would have it. It is also a reason for acclaiming a man who dares, in the heart of our modern world, to be a man *dicendi peritus*, who knows how to speak ; I mean a man who not only says what he thinks and thinks what he says, but also a man who thinks. He is not without a certain courage, the modern orator who defends, inch by inch, a position almost abandoned, holding his own at the extremest and most desperate point of the battle waged by the forces of culture against the assault of the barbarians. Perhaps the ungrateful struggle which he is waging—and in which he is not always supported as he should be by the other combatants—is one of the most necessary of conflicts. For even if there was a time when the artisans of the intellect had to denounce the excesses of speech and of oratorical thought (when Bacon, Descartes, Pascal were wresting a more incisive thought from the matrix of scholastic discourse), now, on the contrary, things have come to such a pass that a rehabilitation of speech might seem almost imperative in the name of the intellect. It is strange that we should have to recall the fact that *discourse* was formerly almost synonymous with *reason* ; and that the Greeks, who knew what they were about, had only one word to express the two notions : *logos*.

VI

It is generally admitted nowadays that lyrical inspiration excludes eloquence ; to speak of the rhetorical gifts of a poet is to depreciate him.

But people did not always think so. Quintilian, who was long the sovereign and undisputed authority in the field of criticism, distinguishes the two styles, and affirms that Lucan, for example, is definitely too oratorical for a poet, "magis oratoribus quam poetis imitandus" (*De Arte oratorio*, X, I, 90). But he does not fail to admire, in all the great Greek and Latin poets, the majesty of their diction and the vigour of their phrasing, and their study is one of those which he considers conducive to the formation of a good orator. In respect of our own literature, the war-cry against eloquence was first sounded by Verlaine : "Take eloquence and wring its neck." But let this be noted ; this was also the period when the poet abdicated his *social* function, a fact on which the Romantics openly congratulated themselves. The art of the symbolists was divorced from the community, and the youthful Verhaeren declared, in a letter to René Ghil : "One writes for oneself alone." Now, it is in the logic of things that the poet, at this stage, repudiates the oratorical act, since this—as we have said—is a social act.

But this is not the logic of which the poet is conscious, and which dictates his refusal. He repudiates eloquence only in the name of sincerity. Yet were his predecessors, throughout so many centuries, strangers to sincerity ? Nevertheless, in our present epoch, eloquence has *become* factitious. It has become factitious because the social and civil order has begun to disintegrate. This is why, by virtue of sincerity, the lyrical muse rejected, with a simple shrug of the shoulders, the social content of poetry (morality !) and the oratorical qualities. Is the innovation a fruitful one in respect of the art of poetry ? In respect of society, above all, it is a disquieting symptom, and in respect of the civilization based upon society.

ELOQUENCE ON TRIAL

VII

A young poet wrote to me : "Under the laudable pretext of wringing the neck of eloquence our epoch has contrived to lose the lyrical sense." Precisely ; except that it would perhaps be more correct to say : "If our epoch is so eager to twist the neck of eloquence it is because it has lost the lyrical sense."

The question is to determine where eloquence begins, where lyricism ends. Whether we like it or not, the two styles are related. Are not the "rhetorical figures" of which the old professors used to speak above all poetical figures, and shall we not find more abundant examples of them in the poets than in the orators ? We might, of course, distinguish lyricism from eloquence by saying that the first spontaneously gives rise to the "rhetorical figures," while the second reproduces them in cold blood, in accordance with the approved recipes. Lyricism would then be none other than the "true eloquence" of which Pascal speaks, that which "disdains eloquence". But the limit is difficult to trace. Every language has to be learned, and that of lyricism like the rest. It calls for a proportion of spontaneous instinct, but also for a proportion of attainment and labour ; let us say, if you will, for one part of pure lyricism and one part of eloquence. If we were really to kill the eloquence in the lyricism, would not that be to reduce this to the cry of an animal ? This could be a literary theory, like many another. Who would wish to uphold anthropoidism ? Even more absurd "issues" have found supporters.

But our epoch does not feel impelled to bay the moon. While it makes a dead set at eloquence, it claims, at the same time, to profess an intellectual and mannered art which is the very antipodes of instinctive expression, and the romantics are blamed for this as much as they are blamed for their rhetoric ! Unhappy poets ! Whether they call a thing black or white, they are always in the wrong ! Give a dog a bad name and drown it . . .

In short, our contemporaries, when they condemn eloquence, do not oppose it to instinctive expression, as a bogus lyricism contrasted with an authentic lyricism (as did Verlaine). But they

87

put eloquence and instinctive expression into the same bag, and it is this bag that they throw into the water. Let us be candid; the dog they want to drown is not eloquence—an artificial lyricism—it is lyricism itself. In these shameless days what prevents them from plainly admitting the fact? One would understand them better. And those who want poetry would look for it elsewhere. At least this would be a saving of time, which in these days is not to be despised.

VIII

If our epoch has such a dislike of eloquence, is not this precisely —amongst other reasons—because it is always pressed for time? This is certainly one reason why it asks for "direct expression," sobriety, conciseness, the amputation of all superfluity (without prejudice to all that we have said of the taste for the "clean sweep"). But let it beware. Art is luxury and leisure, poetry is superfluous, and lyricism has never been sober; it is dionysiacal, overflowing, or it is nothing. The choice must be made.

Art, and the whole of culture, is in the same case as health: that too demands a certain leisure. Our contemporaries will not admit that they are leading a life which is killing them. Perhaps they regard health also as a superfluity? It is a fact that the health of the worker has little effect on the output of the machine.

Yet as a rule our modern folk are more ambitious. They claim that while they lead the life they are leading they still have a right to health. But this is asking too much. And it is asking too much to expect, while leading this life, to retain the sense of poetry and culture. Culture! They have as little culture as silence. The soil in which they grow produces only barbarians. But unfortunately these barbarians have learnt to read—and, what is worse, to write.

XII

OF READING

I

"Cum libro in angulo," says the venerable author of the *Imitation*. "With a book in a corner." But the Latin text says it much better. It rolls out the sonorous words like a plain-chant, with a sort of mystical delectation. Those who know how to read will understand them. Reading is a refuge, a retreat. Does one not enter into reading as one enters into religion ? It is an initiation ; it has its laymen. There are today many such. They read all day long, yet they will never read.

II

Of course, there is no question of preaching a harsh austerity ; no one will think it an offence to seek a "distraction" in reading. But let there be no misunderstanding. Distraction excludes a certain tension, a certain exertion ; it does not exclude all effort, as we perceive in our games, and as children are well aware. (Children know everything, and when they undertake to read they know how to read.) Of course, reading becomes a relaxation only if you have not to rack your brains while reading in order to raise yourself to the height of the book you propose to enjoy ; in other words, if your previous culture sets you more or less on a level with it. On the other hand, let us not be apprehensive of a certain degree of effort, as of one playing a game ; let us allow that the book, even when we ask it to distract us, may exercise the mind as a walk or an outdoor game exercises our muscles, and that it helps to round off our culture. Let us beware of resorting, under the pretext of relaxation, to reading which is definitely beneath our level, and unworthy of us. By so doing it is easy to form bad habits, and the result will presently show itself in a decline of our culture, an increasing incapacity to enjoy works of superior merit.

III

We are on the wrong track directly we begin to seek in books, not a sane and active distraction, but a "pastime" (as though time did not pass of itself !) ; merely something to clap upon boredom in order to fill a gap. To begin with, you ought not to be bored, and there ought not to be a gap. If you are bored it is because you are intellectually ill-bred ; you need re-educating; come back, and we will speak of the matter again ! As for the gaps, they can be patched with care and diligence ; one does not try to fill them at random with just anything.

A collection of books bore the title : "To read in the train !" Another retorted with the title : "To read in the bath !" There you have it ; you open the tap of words and let them run, finding them rather tepid. Such titles are deplorable.

Those in search of a "pastime" will naturally prefer light and futile literature, and there are authors who cater for such readers. I confess that I find it difficult to understand them. In such reading matter, unsubstantial and devoid of beauty, I have never found relaxation, but only a source of irritation. Do I need to relax ? I prefer to close my eyes ; or to open them on the varying greens of the landscape.

V

Before opening a trivial and harmless book think of all the essential books you have not read.

VI

They read the newspapers. And they have read neither Dante, nor Montaigne, nor Goethe. And they do not die of shame ! "This will kill that." One will recall Hugo's brilliant development of this theme in *Notre-Dame de Paris* ; how with the introduction of printing there was bound to be a shifting of the means of expressing thought; the book would kill architecture, and especially the cathedral, that book of stone. Today we have reason to ask ourselves once more : will this kill that ? Will radio kill the book ? But it does not give us what the book gives : the most intimate and secret of dialogues, the voice of another person speaking to himself, the continual invitation to meditation. So it by no means follows that it will kill the book. It is true that it threatens the book—unless measures are taken—and not so much because "listening-in" subtracts "material time" from reading. There is a more serious reason ; there is a danger that exists in the very essence of radio ; a danger inherent in the passiveness which it requires, the continuous delivery, the "open tap," which allows for no pause, no turning back, no questioning : all of which the book permits and demands. And there is reason to fear that those who are too well educated to be "dear listeners," and listeners who do not even listen, yet nevertheless allow themselves to pronounce the complacent "you have just heard"—there is reason to fear that these people, tomorrow, will open their books with the same passivity and indifference—in short, that they will no longer be able to read. For to read is to think. And they . . .

VII

One must not say too much against the radio, for people did not have to wait for that before forgetting how to read (or think). Before the radio there was the cinema, and before the cinema there was the newspaper, which already contained all the poison of which we complain ; and which acted, for analogous reasons, in the same way. It taught readers to forget how to read just as it taught writers to forget how to write ; because it exists for the passing moment : "Latest news, latest edition !" In the eyes of the press the "later" a thing is, the more it is worth. So one hurries on to the last line ; one does not turn back ; and this is the precise antithesis of reading, since reading is a "retreat". And if people thus habituated are interested in Mauriac—for example—

they will be interested in "the latest Mauriac," not so much because it is Mauriac, as because it is "the latest."

Stendhal asks somewhere whether the press, in the modern world, will succeed in replacing the preacher to the edification of the people. He doubts it; but what amazes us is that he could have asked the question seriously; and our astonishment measures precisely how far the press has declined between his day and our own. Is the press to be blamed for this decline? The press is what the period is; there is solidarity between them. We must not blame only the corruption which has been so often denounced; we must also realize that our epoch is the age of haste. But the two things are one and the same. The vice of the daily press is none other than the vice of our epoch. It is the misfortune of the press that it is pressed for time. This is why it cannot, even if it would, be either exact or honest, and why, for the crowds that depend on it for their sole nourishment, it is the worst possible education, whether of the heart or of the intellect. You will tell me that people read a great many books as well. Yes, but a trust of American publishers recently decided that it would be necessary to reduce the price of books to that of the magazines, if they did not wish the magazines to kill the book trade. But the price is unimportant; it would be necessary to lower also the style and the tone. Albert Thibaudeau observed one day that modern prose no longer pays any attention to rhythm, or imagery, or even correctitude; and that it is tending toward the style of the newspaper. The eminent critic made only one mistake; this was, to record the fact calmly, as a mere item of literary history. To maintain the historical and "objective" standpoint in respect of certain crimes against the intellect is the worst *"trahison des clercs."*

Fastidious minds cannot endure the newspapers, or at least, the newspapers as we generally know them; and this for two reasons, given by the astonishing Marie Bashkirtseff—in 1884, and she might have been writing today!—"As for the newspapers, I cannot read three lines of them without disgust. *Not only because their French is a cookery-book French, but because of the ideas . . .* there is nothing genuine about them ! Everything is stipulated or paid for !" (It is true that there are noble spirits in journalism, who have to live by it and in it, who would like to improve it, and do improve it, but they suffer great tribulations !) It is painful to reflect that the mental nutriment of the people should be of such a quality, and that such reading matter should be the outcome of free and compulsory education. Formerly only a few people could read, and they understood only the Bible and the almanac. Then came "the century of enlightenment" ; and people no longer read the Bible, but the "horrible details" of the "latest" crime, or, what is worse, of the last boxing match. The century of enlightenment thought, not without reason, apparently, that it was a good thing to furnish the people's minds, not only with the names of the Evangelists and the Saints of the calendar, but with those of the "great men" to whom the "grateful country" owes its Pantheon. But the devil has taken a hand in the business, as he does in everything. The result is that the people no longer know the names of the saints or the great men, but only those of the "latest" boxers and film stars. "Yet another century of readers," Nietzsche prophesied, "and even the spirit will smell bad." Alas, we had not to wait a century !

IX

The fact is that if "the dead make haste" the living, in our days, are no whit behind. It is their haste, their "press," that has sanctioned "the end of the eternal". But are they not beginning to feel that the temporal has no value save in terms of the eternal ? And that to chase after time as they do is infallibly to lose it ? There are some encouraging symptoms : I will give only one example. I cannot say that I am an infatuated admirer of Proust. But it delights me that there should have been a Proust, and that people admire him. I applaud when I see our hurrying people conceive—even as a matter of snobbishness—a passion for this deliberate, painstaking and insistent author, who takes his time, and who, precisely by dint of deliberation, dawdling, discursiveness, and reminiscence, has recovered *"le temps perdu"*. (Here we have the exact antipodes of the pastime !) That these readers love Proust shows that they have at least a sense of what they lack, and that they too seek to recover their lost time. And is not our time—I mean our age—is it not perhaps irremediably . . . lost ?

XIII

TECHNIQUE VERSUS MYSTICISM.

I

I AM tempted to distinguish five states of mind-stuff, or, if you prefer, five climates of the mind. They form a continuous series, from mysticism to technique. The terms mysticism, lyricism, thought, objectivity, technique, define them well enough. To these states would correspond respectively the activities which these words denote: religion, art, philosophy, science, industry.

One may readily recognize the principle of this arrangement: it moves from the interior to the exterior, from the spiritual to the material, from the intensive to the extensive.

II

If we think of the magical activity of the primitives, and reflect that this activity has been described as a technique which is also a mysticism, we shall see that in magic the two extremities of the series are present and in contact. In other words, the entire spirit is present in magic, but there it exists in a concentrated and undifferentiated form. The evolution of the spirit during the centuries of culture was a process of separating and extending what was massed together. It was the unfolding of a fan. Then the intermediary terms appear.

III

How is this unfolding brought about? If we align from left to right the five terms, proceeding from mysticism to technique, each term seems the more readily to detach itself from the term on its left in proportion as it is attracted by the term on its right; and in spite of various movements and eddies, it seems that the current tends to flow from left to right, from mysticism towards technique : as though mysticism were the igneous centre, the fertile nebula, whence the other terms are expelled, one by one, as they assume their shape. We clearly see mysticism flowering into poetry, and this developing into wisdom ; wisdom expands into science, and science breaks up into an infinite number of techniques.

IV

This, at least, is the view which, explicit or implicit, has impressed itself on our contemporaries ; but even supposing it to be irreproachable, it leads them to false interpretations. They conclude that mysticism is the primitive term and technique the most highly evolved ; and as they understand that evolution is progress, their esteem for the various terms increases as one moves towards the right, and they feel only a condescending disdain for the first terms on the left. This view is mistaken, and is soon seen to be so if we remember that technique was, as a matter of fact, fundamental from the beginning. All that we have a right to say is that technique has derived from mysticism, and that this was progress for technique ; but one must see that at the same time mysticism has been purified of all that has broken away from it ; a decisive stage of this purification being marked by the abandonment of utilitarian prayer, as proposed by Jesus (in Chapter VI of the Gospel according to St. Matthew) : "For your Father knoweth what things ye have need of before ye ask him." And this purification is evidently progress for mysticism.

V

"Hold both ends of the chain." Yet this is not quite what is needed ; for they are not equivalent. But the upper end must be firmly fastened, and fixed at a good height. Do you want to climb a rope ladder ? It must be firmly attached to the beam overhead. This, you say, does not interest you ; all that you wish to do is to ascend to this or that rung, and not to the top. So be it, but you cannot fix the ladder in the empty air at any level that may suit you. You must fasten it overhead, even if you wish to climb only half-way up it. Being firmly fixed, it will hold fast under your effort. Otherwise the whole thing will immediately fall to the ground.

VI

You are regarded as a retrograde person if you denounce the excesses and misdeeds of technique. Technique, you will be told, is not the enemy of the soul. And it certainly is not, any more than the pole is the enemy of the equator. But one cannot be everywhere at the same time, and if one is installed at the pole one cannot keep warm, and if one wishes to return to the equator one has to pass through the intermediate climates; all those "zones" so clearly depicted in our school atlas. I have sometimes told the story of the boy who, with exceptional ability, built for himself a radio transmitter, combined with a phonograph; and when he had completed his apparatus it never occurred to him to reproduce anything but jazz. This boy is a compact symbol of the grandeur and misery of the modern Occident, equipped with its technique, and with it so perfectly representing a "world without a soul".

VII

The slope descending from mysticism to technique is properly the gradient of the modern spirit; it has equipped itself with technique in a kind of frenzy. Levy-Brühl was thinking as a modern man when for a moment he was tempted to define as "mystical" the primitive mentality for which he has now happily adopted the term "prelogical". This magical stage of primitive man is mystical from the standpoint of the empty technique which is ours, for it represents a technique charged with mysticism. But seen from the other end, from the standpoint of a purified and disinterested mysticism, this same state might be as justly defined as technique, for it represents a mysticism encumbered with practical recipes and practical ability.

THE MYTH OF MODERNITY

VIII

The peculiar misuse of the term "a mysticism" of late years is a linguistic phenomenon worthy of remark, which doubtless conceals a psychological phenomenon.

It is, of course, the destiny of words to wear out and be withdrawn from circulation ; but here the degradation of the term has been altogether too quick and brutal. Not only do people speak of nationalistic or revolutionary mysticisms, which is understandable ; but now, if we are to believe the journalists, we have the mysticism of sport, competition, youth, muscle, jazz—and what have you ! They barely refrain from discoursing upon the mysticism of petroleum, rubber, and magazines at a standard price. Lastly, there is of course a mysticism of technique, which completes the looping of the loop and turns everything topsy turvy.

The exaltations to which the term mysticism is applied do not in any sense deserve it, yet this degradation of the word must have a meaning. Is it not to be found in a certain nostalgia for a true mysticism, in a secular desire that is making itself felt everywhere ? By this degradation of the term one world expresses eloquently how little it has of the thing, and how this lack of the thing has become an obsession.

IX

There are those who today, speaking in the name of science, consider that philosophy is superannuated ; but they (or their sons, or their disciples) will conclude tomorrow that theoretical science is superannuated, and will profess to reduce science to technique. They may also understand, if they reflect on the matter, that to reject philosophy is to amputate science, and, going a step further, they may finally realize that to renounce mysticism is to compromise all the rest.

XIV

A MODERATE VIEW OF HAPPINESS

I

MONSIEUR BOUTOURLINE, that Russian character of the *ancien régime* whose portrait Maurice Kuès has drawn in his *Initiation moscovite*, is an agreeable talker and an indulgent philosopher. Other talkers fascinate their audience by the violence of their paradoxes. He holds our attention by the moderation of his opinions. But as we are living in times that deal in extremes and paroxysms, it so happens that moderation, provided we find it on the lips of a man of intellect, will itself figure as a paradox and will charm us for that very reason.

Monsieur Boutourline does not think that human beings can be very happy. We suspected as much! But how does he express himself? He tells us of his belief in a manner that has no suggestion of pessimism, nor does it incline us to pessimism. On the contrary!

"What is a happiness that one cannot attain?" asks the doctor who is conversing with our hero. And he replies:

"But, my dear fellow, where have you found that a happiness was ever attained?"

"It is true," says the doctor, "that I have never found it in anyone, and those who say they have found it are like characters in a novel, who deceive one, and deceive themselves."

"Happiness cannot be attained, and we do not encounter it; but the notion we have of it is indispensable to human life. If a man did not aspire to happiness he would be only half alive."

The discussion continues, pleasantly varied by little incidents which are observed with irony under the aspect of happiness. Or are they merely sensual delights?

Finally, it is Monsieur Boutourline who figures, as always, and without pedantry, as the spokesman of the sagest wisdom :

"But it is precisely because we are not happy that we long for happiness, and believe that it will come tomorrow. If we had not this hope which of us would care to live? Our vital energy is none other than the expectation of happiness, our faith in happiness.

"Happiness . . . It comes into our hearts with every pulse of blood that is regenerated there and returns to the farthest extremities of our bodies with a fresh promise. Happiness is not a state ; it is really a promise, renewed every moment."

II

One day we recalled to mind an anecdote of Amiel, who, when he felt attracted by a young woman, began a kind of book-keeping by double entry, in order to determine whether her good qualities showed a credit balance over her faults, so that he might decide, mathematically, whether it would be expedient for him to marry her. Naturally, we said, he never married.

This was an attempt to apply arithmetic where it was out of place. But it is the besetting sin of speculative minds to attempt to reduce everything to a calculation, and they are constantly giving way to it. Montesquieu, in his *Cahiers*, alludes to a certain "balance of pleasures and pains" imagined by his contemporary M. de Maupertuis, a distinguished naturalist and geometrician, who perhaps was rather too much the geometrician in so naïvely investigating the natural history of man. The system of the "arithmetic of pleasure" was to be applied again by Bentham, who derived from it a morality rather too like a system of book-keeping.

But while our common sense usually warns us that we must observe a sceptical prudence in approving such attempts, we should generally find it rather difficult to explain the motives of our distrust. Montesquieu, with the calm perspicacity of which he has elsewhere given us so many proofs, puts his finger on the defect of the system :

"M. de Maupertuis includes in his calculation only pleasures and pains ; that is to say, all that apprizes the soul of its happiness or unhappiness. He does not include the happiness of existence and the habitual felicity which apprizes us of nothing, because it it habitual." (p. 26).

The meaning of this criticism is that happiness is not the total of a sum of events capable of enumeration ; it is a state. The events stand out against the background which is painted by this state ; they colour it and accentuate it, but do not make it. It would be better to call it a *disposition* rather than a state. Does not happiness consist above all in a disposition to welcome it ? On the whole, does not a man possess a happy nature rather than a happy destiny ? At least one must conclude that his nature determines the tone of his destiny.

"In a favourable disposition," says Montesquieu, "such accidents as wealth, honours, health and sickness increase or diminish happiness. On the contrary, in an unfavourable disposition accidents increase or diminish unhappiness." (p.17).

III

Happiness is "a promise perpetually renewed." the curious fact is that the formula may appear equally depressing or encouraging. All depends on the tone in which it is expressed ; once again, it is the tune that makes the song. If people would understand that the moral truths are in the first place poetical truths they would profit greatly.

"What is a promise perpetually renewed ?" the disgruntled critic will ask. To renew it is to devalue it ; it is to undermine confidence. Such renewal is good enough for pacts of friendship between States, for obligatory oaths of fidelity, and other simulacra of a political order, which are neither closely nor distantly related to the moral life, and which are very displeasing when they profane its language. A promise perpetually renewed is, when all is said, a bad joke ; it is precisely like the promise of the famous barber : "Tomorrow customers are shaved gratis." This barber, continues the gloomy critic, according to your Boutourline, might just as well have inscribed on his shopfront : "At the sign of Happiness !"

But this dismal person is prosaic. And the prosaic man, by definition, is one who understands nothing. A promise perpetually renewed may not mean very much if reduced to logical terms. But if we listen to these words with our poetical sense they mean a great deal. They recall the matutinal promise lavished upon us and indefatigably repeated, day by day, by the dawn ; a promise to which we have often attempted to respond.

Happiness—*bonheur*—is a promise. This formula has the merit of introducing into our notion of happiness the sense of time. Or rather, of reminding us that time is included in the promise, for it is inscribed in the very structure of the word. It is inscribed otherwise than we imagine, for the generations have misconstrued the word, and the *heur* of *bonheur* comes, it seems, from *augurium*, which very precisely denotes a promise ; while we understand it as *hora*, and the misconception is contained in this superfoetatory "e". It is of no importance. In *bonheur* as well as in *malheur* we have the word *heure* ; so, when we think of happiness, we think of a privileged moment. Thus, the common notion of happiness is not, after all, so optimistic ; it admits the possibility of a momentary flowering or maturity. And when, after this, one speaks of an absolute happiness which would endure forever, is not one introducing a sort of contradiction in terms ? "O Time, suspend thy flight !" But what is a time that does not fly ? Let us admit that in what we say of happiness, as in what we say of time, there is a good deal of verbalism.

IV

We shall be less surprised by this if we recall what Bergson has taught us with such subtlety ; that language was not created for temporal—or, as he would prefer to say—enduring things ; that the misunderstandings of language give rise, in this connection, to many contradictions and spurious problems, which baffle the intelligence, and which life alone, impelled by instinct and confident in its own powers, is able to overcome, if not resolve. Now, happiness is of the temporal order. We are told that it is a promise rather than a state (a good *augury* !). We will say, if you prefer it : a becoming and not a thing.

Directly we express a mental attitude by a word we imagine that a thing corresponds to this word, for we are accustomed to seek a correspondence. This is a bad habit acquired from our first school reading-book, in which there were pretty coloured pictures of things, and a name under each picture. But this happens only in the material world. In the moral life it may happen that the word corresponds only with an attitude of the mind. Thus it is with happiness, *bonheur*. It is not proven that there is anything which to the challenge of this word is bound to reply : Present! As for us, expecting a thing and not finding it, we are disappointed. This is how disillusion and pessimism are born, as well as the mirages of progress which project happiness into the future. But have we not been the dupes of language ? And we are wrong ; for in our disappointment we reason as though where there is no thing there is nothing at all. But an attitude of the mind is perhaps more important than a thing.

We escape from this confusion if we can contrive to think of happiness not in a static but in a dynamic manner ; to think of it as an aspiration and not as a fact ; as a direction and not as a place ; as a fine and gracious gesture by which life points out our path.

V

Now that we seem to understand why there are so many misunderstandings as soon as anyone speaks of happiness, we shall be readier to confront, without being completely baffled, the contradictory statements of various thinkers in this connection.

We have enjoyed such a diverting skirmish between M. Boutourline and the wise Alain. There is no longer any agreement between them—or so it seems at the first glance. There is no happiness, said the first, save that which is not realized, but promised and expected. The second, who would rather hold his ground than run, writes, with the sound sense of a working-man: "Happiness is not something that one runs after, but something that one possesses. Apart from this possession it is only a word." (*Quatre-vingt-un chapitres sur les passions*, V, 1).

Are we to oppose these opinions and lose ourselves in polemics? Rousseau has already warned us that nothing could be more foolish. And Alain himself, in the preface to his book, guides us in Rousseau's footsteps. "I do not believe," he says, "that any important portion of theoretical and practical philosophy is omitted from what follows, apart from polemics that teach no one anything."

If one wishes to profit from the lessons of the sages, or merely from the teaching of human beings, one must admit that contraries have the same civic rights in the temple of Truth, where the statue of Minerva is seen, now full-face, now in profile, so that one might at first believe that there were two hostile statues, especially since both are armed. And suddenly one sees that the two images correspond. In the same chapter of Alain's (on Happiness) I read again: "There is nothing that pleases if one receives it, and hardly anything that does not please if one makes it... A garden does not give pleasure unless one has made it. A woman does not please unless one has conquered her. Even power wearies him who has obtained it without effort."

Here is happiness expressed in terms of action. Happiness, one may say, is not so much something that one possesses as something that one has created. (Or one may say that one truly possesses only that which one creates.) It is not a state, but an act. And so we find our way back to the dynamism, the becoming, of which the other wise man told us. The discord is resolved.

A MODERATE VIEW OF HAPPINESS

VI

OASIS

Measure life no longer
By the tally of the days.

In the heartbreaking desert,
In the caravan of the years
There is a blessed hour,
There are restful oases.

Bewail no more the fact
That in the implacable waste
The oasis is only a speck.

For the waste and the speck
Have no kinship, no place of meeting.
The living spot contains in itself
An immensity of bliss.

By virtue of a unique
Geometry, it hollows
An inner dimension,
A concentrated eternity.

There is no arid waste
But a fruitful depth.
It drinks at the very heart of the world
Where the living waters rise.

O minutes, divinely granted,
You are requital enough
For the waste of the arid years.

I will grasp life no longer
By the sum of accursed days.

THE MYTH OF MODERNITY

VII

A water-hole is only a hole ; but it contains water. This correction of perspective is applicable to many of our judgments. We have already suspected that the "arithmetic of pleasures" by which some have attempted a numerical valuation of happiness is a delusion. Is it not so because they forget the other dimension—which, to make the image clearer, we will call the vertical dimension ? A great deal of pessimism is due to forgetfulness of this other dimension—that of height and depth, the two directions for which the Latin tongue had only one word —a beautiful word—*altitudo*.

We are too eager to strike the balance of the happiness that life has brought us ; and if we do it on one of our bad days we are very likely to find that the balance is not there, or that it is pitifully small. And if our fit of sulks is philosophical we decide that we are pessimists, and that it is life itself of which we complain. Or perhaps we expect something only from tomorrow ; or from progress ; from more modern conditions. (The barber's sign !)

But what have we been doing ? We have spread out the past hours, side by side, on a flat surface ; and it is true that the blessed hours fill but a small space. But we have forgotten to lift our eyes, and to look down, in thought ; we have failed to realize that these hours have an exceptional quality, which makes up for their feeble quantity. It is true that on the map Mont Blanc or Mount Everest is shown only as a speck ; the map does not reveal to the eye their 15,000 or 29,000 feet. But in reality this other dimension exists, and is all-important. Two-dimensional judgments are false.

VIII

The judgments that plume themselves on being "modern"—or worse, "realistic"—are commonly two-dimensional judgments.

IX

We move about on the plane of daily life, which is flat as a map ; and thus we fail to realize—like the fly crawling over the

A MODERATE VIEW OF HAPPINESS

map—that mountains have altitude, and that certain moments have a splendour incommensurable with time. This omission, of which each of us is guilty, becomes a professional distortion in the politician ; and his example will enable us the better to grasp the fact. The politician—above all if he aggravates his title by the epithet of realistic—refuses to move except in his own plane. This would be endurable if he were not immediately tempted to imagine that nothing exists outside this plane. He sees it like a chessboard, on which forces represented by points can be measured and combined. Nothing is more disheartening than the total incomprehension of such a man for any spiritual reality.

Napoleon's blindness where Corneille was concerned—though he professed to appraise him so highly—was instinctive. "Not long ago," said Napoleon one day, "I was looking into the *dénouement* of *Cinna*. I could see nothing in it but the means of constructing a pathetic fifth act, and even so, clemency, properly so called, is such a poor little virtue, where it is not based on politics, that the clemency of Augustus, who had suddenly become a good-natured sovereign, did not seem to me worthy of bringing this fine tragedy to a close. But Monvel, once, when he was playing it before me, revealed the whole mystery of this magnificent conception. He pronounced the words ('Let us be friends, Cinna!') in such a clever and cunning tone that I realized that this action was only the pretence of a tyrant, and as calculation I approved of what had seemed to me puerile as sentiment." So, at least, Mme. de Remusat informs us in Chapter IV of the first volume of her *Mémoires*.

One could not imagine a more lamentable misunderstanding. Genius though he may have been on his own plane, a chess-player, he was blind to the third dimension. So is every mere politician, and every historian who judges things as a mere politician. If in the jungle of facts they encounter some sentiment, some great mind, some religious movement, they see in it only one of the pieces of the game, one factor among others ; and they endeavour, because it is simpler, to reduce it to the same denominator as the other pieces, and to measure its effect on the same scale as that applied to a traitor, a conspiracy, or an economic disaster. They see only the plane of incidence, and as for the great vertical factors which pierce it like flaming swords, they see only their points of incidence on the plane. These lines, which are infinite, are in their eyes only points among other points. So it is with all who call themselves realists. They are now and always flies on the map of the world. The world, with its prodigious peaks and ranges, escapes them.

X

"All that is well said," replied Candide, "but we must cultivate our garden." One is fond of quoting the remark which forms the close of Voltaire's sprightly novel. But as with many sayings that are often quoted, one does not always remember the circumstances which led up to it, and one realizes even more rarely the true significance of the words.

It must be remembered that *Candide* is above all the arraignment of systematic optimism. The philosopher Pangloss, even when he sees himself disfigured—when he is shipwrecked—when he is sentenced to death and hanged—and carelessly hanged, for a little later we find him still alive—the philosopher Pangloss always considers that all is for the best in the best of worlds. He wants to teach his optimism to Candide, and to persuade him that even if he has been violently kicked out of the château of the Baron Thunder Ten Tronck as the lover of the fair Cunégonde, all is still for the best in the best of worlds. Candide is only half convinced ; but it must be admitted that he is no more convinced by the discourse of the philosopher Martin, the professional pessimist, who forms a pendant to Pangloss, and he wisely prefers to conclude that "we must cultivate our garden".

What does this mean ? It actually represents an original attitude toward the problem of evil. It is, if you will, a decision to transpose the problem from the intellectual plane to the plane of action. On the intellectual plane it is very discouraging. We can hardly understand evil, and if we try to justify it we find it

A MODERATE VIEW OF HAPPINESS

difficult to avoid the contradictions which enable Voltaire's malicious wit to make us look ridiculous. But abandoning these speculations, it is permissible to turn to action, to the humble, immediate, everyday activity in which, without asking ourselves how far the world is good or bad in itself, we can at least hope to make it a little better within the modest radius of our action. It is neither good in itself nor bad in itself, but it is capable of becoming better, and by our efforts; and there we have the philosophy of progress.

Has anyone observed that the conclusion of Candide was to become the conclusion of Faust ? Faust also studied philosophy, to say nothing of various sciences, but they left him as he was in the beginning. So then he turned to life, which rewarded him, as it rewarded Candide and Pangloss, though in a loftier style, with many misadventures. At last he found salvation in action, and, if you will, in a humble action. For if "in the beginning was action," as he says somewhere, action is also at the end. We see him building dykes to wrest from the sea, the irrational and infinite element, a few inches of soil, on which a few human families can in turn . . . cultivate their garden. We must conclude that the advice is not so bad. But as Voltaire always speaks playfully, it is as well to hear it repeated in a more earnest and emotional tone.

XI

The dialectic of Candide, which sums up Voltaire's attitude to the problem of evil (which he turns about and examines from every side on many other occasions) is highly instructive for anyone who wishes to understand the origin of the modern ideologies :

One day will all be well : that is our hope.

That all is well today—that is delusion.

The conjugate ideas of *progress* and *action*—so unforgettably combined in the maxim that we should "cultivate our garden"—are in this system only a reply to the problem of evil or a means of eluding it. Man needs an insurance against evil, and the old idea of *Providence* offers it to him; evil can be neither radical nor final since Providence wills it. Now, in the 18th century, the idea of Providence had lost much of its virtue; man had become the animalcule of *Micromégus* and the *Désastre de Lisbonne*, and when Bernardin de Saint-Pierre, a little later, undertook the defence of Providence, he cut the sorry figure of the man who "wants to prove too much". The man of the 18th century, the Voltairean, sought another insurance against evil. He hit on *progress*, and *action*, which is an inseparable condition of progress. These notions were evoked to deputize for a Providence which was regarded as in default. The seeds of the modern mentality were sown. And this is the meaning of the seemingly inoffensive conclusion of *Candide*.

XII

Towards the end of Flaubert's *Tentation de Saint Antoine* there is a very striking picture. It introduces two fantastic creatures, the Sphinx and the Chimera, to which, if we wanted to translate these appellations, we might give more abstract names, such as Science and Fantasy, or Reason and Imagination. The Sphinx, at a certain moment, asks the winged Chimera to carry her away; and the Chimera consents. The Sphinx mounts on her back, but then the Chimera is crushed under the weight of the Sphinx. Here is a symbol by which one cannot fail to be impressed. Fantasy, on contact with reality, admits that she is an illusion, and loses all consistency. But one may ask whether she is not too readily resigned.

This visionary scene portrays, if we think it over, a stage, and indeed a crisis, in the history of thought. The stage is the period of Flaubert; the years following 1860; the morrows of the fine Romantic orgy. People had recovered from the orgy; they were sobered. Positivism had done its work and had conquered many minds. Science no longer permitted the existence, in the real world, of those unexplored continents in which fantasy could sport at will. Then fantasy decided to surrender to reality, and this decision, in art, was known as realism. But realism, in the end, is the crushing of the Chimera under the weight of the other Beast.

Is this the last word ? By no means ! Since then, thank God, we have seen the Chimera recover herself and rebel. Symbolism might stand for this revolt. At the same time a whole philosophical movement made itself apparent, reaffirming, beyond reason and science, the rights of intuition and belief. In fact, a new dimension had to be recognized, in which the Chimera could once more disport herself, and, as we say, "take a hair of the dog that bit her".

Realism should not have the last word in any domain ; it is in the nature of the mind to refuse its consent to this privilege. It will get out of the predicament as best it can ; but at any cost the winged creature that Flaubert calls the Chimera, and for which one ought perhaps to seek a less unflattering name, must not allow itself to be crushed. If this crisis has its place in history it has also repeated itself in the individual consciousness. The moment comes, for everyone, when such a chimera is crushed under the weight of reality. But may this never be the end of the matter !

XIII

A question which has been debated in all ages by the sages and philosophers is the question of the sovereign good. The very different answers which the question has received are typical of the various schools of philosophy and morality, which debate matters between themselves, sometimes with courtesy and sometimes with violence and acrimony ; in which they show that they are not so wise as they pretend, and do themselves no less discredit than the master of philosophy in *Le Bourgeois Gentilhomme*, who comes to blows with the other masters in order to prove the excellence of his doctrine.

What we should learn from the divergence of views as to the sovereign good is not a vain scepticism, but, once more, relativity. Perhaps the most reasonable solution would be to agree that there is no such thing in this world as a sovereign good, but that a good appears most desirable to us at the moment when we are deprived of it. This simple proposition may be of great assistance to us if we are inclined to feel discouraged by the thought that it is precisely the highest good of which we have been deprived. But no, we must not say precisely, and we must not speak as though we had been deprived of it by the malice of destiny. Is it not rather simply because it has escaped as that it appears the highest good ?

XIV

This suggests a little poem of Victor Hugo's, at the beginning of his *Contemplations* :

>'Tis true : all men are weary of their lot.
>For all men to be glad—O sorry fate !
>One thing is lacking, one thing is forgot ;
>   Some thing of little weight.
>
>It is this little thing that men by stealth
>Seek through the world, and still desire the while :
>A word, a name, a glance, a little wealth,
>   Perchance a smile.
>
>What lacks the mighty king who loves not ?   Mirth.
>What lacks the desert waste ?   A drop of rain . . .

Does not this mean—one may be asked—that the world is badly arranged ?   Is it not diabolical that we always value *precisely* (we always come back to that *precisely*) what we have not ?

Yet it is natural, if we come to think of it—yet it is logical that a sense of value should be attributed to the action which our organism is preparing itself to perform ; as we see clearly in the operation of the instincts.   Now, the action for which a properly constituted organism should at every moment be prepared is the action calculated to defend and preserve it, to supply the want which might be prejudicial to it.   It is natural and useful that we should suffer pain "precisely" in the affected organ.   And here

A MODERATE VIEW OF HAPPINESS

the word "precisely" changes its meaning ; it no longer hints at the perverse combinations of malicious chance ; it signifies that the location is just, or, so to speak, adjusted, in a sense which evokes the laws of adaptation of the living organism.

On the whole, it is just, it is "precisely" right, that we should want what we have not, for if we had it, it would no longer be necessary to want it, and Nature, they say, does nothing in vain. But let us stop here, or we shall end by meeting M. de la Palisse.

XV

The simple observation of the great natural rhythms leads to meditation, which soothes the mind. Even the quotidian cycle of the sun is instructive and beneficent to consider, and men who live close to Nature can consider it at greater leisure and derive a greater benefit.

We will say nothing against clockmaking, which is a very fine thing, and which, like all honest trades, teaches us valuable lessons ; but let us sometimes give a thought to the old makers of sundials, and to the charming mottos with which they adorned their handiwork, inspired by a wisdom which seemed natural to them, and was doubtless dictated by the movements of the regal and tranquil star whose habits they observed. *Horas non numero, nisi serenas*, said one of these sundials ; which might be translated thus : "I number only the cloudless hours." A *jeu d'esprit*, if you like, but it is full of poetry.

Why is the author of this maxim unknown to us ? He must have had a witty mind, or at least what we call a happy nature. This motto exhales a sunny and peaceful generosity which is rare ; for it must be confessed that we are more inclined to grumble than to give thanks. This is obvious even from our relations with our fellows ; we are readier to remember insults than presents. And if we tend to personify destiny, it is only to repeat in our attitude toward destiny our disagreeable relations with our fellow-men. We are always accusing fate, as the peasant accuses the weather, and we are slow to acknowledge the favours of a lucky star.

Why is this, if it is not that we implicitly believe that everything is due to us? And whence comes this naïve belief, if it is not a survival of our earliest infancy, when we had always watching over us a maternal and tutelary power, ready to anticipate all our needs?

What if we learned to correct this tendency? If we tried no longer to insist on the injuries inflicted on us, on the misfortunes that befall us, but rather to gather with the patience of a gleaner the golden straws scattered about our path? If in the evening, or at break of day, as one makes an examination of one's conscience, we were to strike the balance of the little joys of the day, or of yesterday? Then, no doubt, we should give thanks, even on our darkest days, when, by contrast, the smallest grains of joy shine with a more than common and more precious lustre.

XV

THE PARADOXES OF EDUCATION

I

CHANGE man in order to change society ; change society in order to change man ; these two recipes are in constant opposition.

II

I know of nothing more foolish than the superior shrug of the shoulders of those politicians who regard any appeal to the individual as Utopian, while on the other hand they regard themselves as realists because they speak of ameliorating social conditions. After all, there is one crucial experience : it is this—that we cannot name any society, great or small, which is not very imperfect, while we can point to pure and noble individuals, as close as you like to the highest ideal that one can form of human beings ; there are saints, but there are no holy cities. It seems to me that here we have the proof that however difficult it may be to improve the individual, it is less difficult than to ameliorate society. This is a very strong argument in favour of education.

III

The partisans of the primacy of social affairs have the advantage, however, in so far as they are able to prove, on the authority of Durkheim, that every *ideal* is a creation of the social order. The saint, they will say, is an individual ; but the ideal on which he models himself to become a saint has been furnished by the beliefs and inspirations of the society in which he lives. Thus, it would be a function of society to posit the ideal, which it is incapable of realizing itself, and which can only be embodied in individuals. This formula would do justice to both principles.

IV

But the social environment would then have to inspire men with an authentic ideal. We know that it does secrete myths; and it proposes to the individual an end in conformity with the ideology of these myths. That is all. But before this end could be indisputable one would have to extend the sociological metaphysic to the point of denying any criterion but the social; which would be extremely rash. The end is worth what the myth from which it proceeds is worth. If the myth proposed by society is excellent, education will not be going outside its province in trying to embody it in the individual; and all will be as it should be. But if the social myth is definitely inferior and regressive, if it is positively barbaric, how should education react against it? Can it react against it? To what authority will it appeal?

V

The experiment of the "new school" has sometimes had quite unforeseen results. Even persons who are otherwise in favour of the experiment quite readily express their uneasiness in respect of one particular point. "Yes, yes," they say, "but later on, when these children, educated in freedom, have to enter a university, a workshop, an office, when at last they will be subjected to discipline, will they be able to adapt themselves to the necessary formality, to the detestable but inescapable constraints?" Now, there are cases when things happen quite otherwise than one had expected. We are now beginning to see some of these children who have been subjected to the whole experiment, and their parents tell me: "There they are, at college, and far from finding themselves at a loss, they adapt themselves immediately; it is positively *startling* (sic) to see how they adapt themselves, and the eagerness with which they become schoolboys among other schoolboys, while they think the only object of their studies is to enable them to pass examinations." One would say that these children, educated in non-conformity, have but one aspiration—on the first opportunity to become more conformist than the others. As a matter of fact, this is natural; one ought to have foreseen it; in this they are asserting themselves against the norm of their childhood's environment, which is what every growing child tends to do. If this norm was the very affirmation of the children's personality, they would then show that they asserted it by rejecting this very affirmation, and by cultivating the most deplorable conventionality. This does not condemn the experiment; but it gives us reason to think that it ought to have been carried farther, and that in this case an environment in which conformism prevailed would not necessarily offer such an irresistible temptation to these children.

VI

It is owing to a somewhat similar mechanism that the children of distinguished persons are so often disappointing and ordinary. Their destiny, to tell the truth, is rather tragic. They aspire, like all children, to assert themselves against their parents (more especially the son against the father, the daughter against the mother). When the parents are eminent personalities do not the children (other things being equal) run a greater risk than others of realizing this assertion of themselves—by force of contrast—in mediocrity?

VII

Here is food for thought. This is what one may fear: Let us take a child educated, in whatever fashion, in a closed vessel, in some especially select and excellent school; he himself becomes, not perhaps an infant prodigy, but an exceptional scholar, one of the *élite*. Now let him be dropped into the midst of ordinary schoolboys. Superior to the rest, he feels, above all, that he is different. Will he not feel his superiority as a disgrace, and think only of trampling it underfoot, of eliminating all traces of it? In short, will not this child, at his first contact with the wider social environment, from which one has tried to preserve him, now tend to adopt the norms of this environment with a sort of frenzy? (As the youthful Buddha perceived so poignantly, on his first contact with it, the world of sorrow and death which a princely education had sought to save him from perceiving or even suspecting). Is this a child who has been educated in liberty ? Well, if need be he will choose a Prussian discipline, as the liberation from his inculcated liberty !

VIII

This is what education is up against. This is where its power of correcting the environment meets with its unforeseen and obstinate limitation. The environment is powerful, we admit ; it is all-powerful. However delightful school may be made for him, the child looks out of the window, and there he sees the environment from which his elders want to save him. On the first opportunity he will fling himself into it and adopt its myths.

IX

It is only too easy to see that in order to change the myths secreted by the environment, and thus the environment itself, one must have men. Then we think of making men ; we think of education. But the environment is on its guard. Will it not recapture these men all the more eagerly because we have tried to set them against it ? Let us confess the truth : the devil has a hand in the business, and the devil is strong.

X

Is there no weak point through which one can escape from the circle ? The truth is that one escapes when the environment changes of itself, by reason of far-reaching economic, political and social circumstances which are beyond the reach of human wills. Let us admit, then, however humiliating it may be, that one escapes only by chance.

XI

It would be possible to take another point of view. We find that education goes astray because it stops at a given moment, and at this moment the social environment assumes control. It goes astray because it is only a child's education, a pedagogy. Should there not also be a constant education of the adult : what we are beginning to call a *psychogogy* ? In other ages this education was the undisputed function of the Churches. If their formula is discredited—even among those who profess themselves to be believers—it must be rejuvenated. The education is essential, and it is evident that it does not exist.

XII

We are returning, today, to individual psychogogy, by a quite unexpected détour, and at one narrowly circumscribed point : in the treatment of the neuroses. When the adult admits that he is ill, and when he can no longer know where to turn, he consents to accept confession, re-education, a director of the conscious, and anything else required of him. And it is impossible to treat the modern neurosis without re-educating the patient in respect of the values which the modern world has forgotten. Neurosis is the salutory warning that the patient is on the wrong track. At the same time, one would not wish to subject everyone to this costly détour. But it is long odds that if the modern man does not consent to perceive for himself the biological errors of which he is guilty then, Nature will undertake to warn him, sooner or later, by her accustomed methods.

XIII

Good conduct is discredited. It is only the child who is asked to "be good" ; in his eyes "being good" is a quality proper to the nursery, so that in his mind "being good" is symmetrically opposed to "being grown up." And as he wants above all to be grown up, he will reject all "goodness," with a shrug of the shoulders, on the first opportunity ; all the more so as "being good" is incompatible with the myths secreted by the modern environment ; speed, record performances, outbidding one's neighbour. And so the circle is tightly closed.

XIV

But fortunately the inverse circle also is closed. Here again the gods avenge themselves. The modern man can conceive no other ideal than performance ; he would jump over his own head if he could. This is why he discards good conduct, which is *moderation*. Very well : but he cannot escape the laws of equilibrium, the return of the pendulum. Nothing is more monotonous than excess. The very conceptions of the modern man make him incurably mediocre, which is another way, though a less desirable one, of returning to the middle point. What is more, he is and proclaims himself to be *modern* above all things, without perceiving that the revenge of the gods is written in this very word, and that in it he encounters the same idea (the same root) that he sought to escape by rejecting all moderation. He is trapped !

XV

Again it will be necessary to teach him, to make him see. Nature is still the great teacher. But he will not find experience enough. He must extract its lessons.

XVI

THE GIFT OF CHILDHOOD

1

A SCULPTOR, having read some of the foregoing ideas, wrote to me as follows :

"I too have put on paper my ideas about life and the world, more or less for the following reasons. I have always been dominated by the love of Nature, an exacting love which soon brought me into conflict with civilization and men, because before them Nature has to sing so terribly small. I tried at first to submit to the fact and to rally to the stronger side, but it was not in my power to do so sincerely. I regarded myself as abnormal, in some way perverse ; I also believed that I was a misanthrope . . . Nevertheless, I continued to observe Nature and to express my observations. And by this I came into touch with people ; better still, they regarded my way of life with respect and often even with envy."

It is by remaining as far as possible faithful to this flouted Nature that one comes into the most direct contact with one's fellow-men, and even those who flout her, and profess that they are utterly and completely modern, mechanized and Taylorized. For they are putting themselves under constraint. Whether they know it or not—as a rule they do not know it—they are acting a part, and a part which they secretly dislike. Under his dull or brilliant carapace remains the natural man, with all his drama and his secret depths. By being simply oneself it may happen that one comes into contact with the man, touching him through some chink in his armour, and if one touches this in the right place it will respond, as certain copper vessels will suddenly begin to vibrate in sympathy. And one has done a little towards setting the captive free.

THE MYTH OF MODERNITY

II

One forces oneself to play an inhuman part, and under this cuirass a whole real and suffering humanity complains and bewails its hard lot.

Could one not say that this profound and secret being is the child ? The child that was once repressed in order to make the man—or to make him a modern man. This being, who was so sensitive, curious, quick, and open to all influences, no longer shows himself; the man on the surface has become brutal and narrow ; he has a trade, and he lives for the sake of gain ; he is the member of a party and repeats its slogans. All this time the child he was is complaining somewhere within him, forgotten, in the dark. But he is there ; and we have only to think of him in order to realize that men are less different than they seem. One may show more of his true being ; another hides it more carefully from his fellows, and from himself ; but if we add the total, in one and the other case, of what is shown and what is concealed, we shall obtain a correct result. This view inclines one to indulgence. This is admirably demonstrated by Charles Morgan, the author of *The Fountain* and *Sparkenbroke*, in a rather less well-known novel : *Portrait in a Mirror*.

"I began to think," he says, "that I should never be able to hate or ridicule any of mankind, if, in imagination, I first shared their childhood with them . . . If each criminal stood his trial in his own nursery there could be neither prison nor gallows . . . A great artist perceives beneath all concealments that innocency of life which is the only background capable of exhibiting the truth of pain, of joy, of each human experience. In the criminal he perceives one who formerly was guiltless ; in the harlot, maidenhood ; in age, youth . . . It is this power of imagination which, if an artist possess it, separates him from other men so that they can see nothing from his point of view. They are not to blame ; they must conduct the world as it is ; they are its administrators, not the givers of truth to it . . . From his power to see children in men sprang that unique quality in Christ's judgment which was not what we call justice nor what we call mercy."

III
CHILDREN'S DRAWINGS

My child,
We have hung on the walls of the house
The drawings you made in your childhood.
Here they are, a pathetic circle,
Tracing about us the ring of a magic horizon.

Mountains are there, and churches,
Suns that rise to a colourful greeting,
A country of legend, and always churches,
And trees which are like great flowers,
And beneath, in the underwood, the home of fairies,
Enormous mushrooms, which are hooded dwarfs.
Your soul is there ; my child, your whole soul.

Later, when you have been among men,
And have succeeded, as best you could
In making yourself in the image of others,
And when you have taken the utmost pains
To be strong, like them—which is to say, brutal,
And smart, like them—which is to say, vulgar,

With the thick skin that is proper for war,
With the dense mind that is proper for man,
And when you have taken the utmost pains
To be no more yourself, to be worse by far,
On a later day,
When you have stoned your soul and driven it off,
Perhaps one day you will meet it again,
Gazing at you with a sad, strange gaze,
From the depth of your drawings hung on the wall,
Like the softly-flying nocturnal birds
The peasants nail on the doors of their byres.

This will be twenty, forty years hence,
Then you will find your deserted soul
Faithfully waiting behind the glass.
Touching it then with an awkward hand,
You will feel its warmth, you will know that it lives,
Like the soft and silent birds of the night
That hide all day in the corniced eaves.
And then you will know that this is the whole, the real you.

IV

There is a nucleus of freshness and childhood which one may find, at last, if one follows the right path of many, under the husk of cynical, hardened and misanthropic characters. We find it in La Rochefoucauld, in the confession contained in a certain phrase relating to love. And in Stendhal. Charles Morgan led us to it just now. As a continuation of his reflections we might turn to one of the touching and truculent poems in *argot* of Jehan Rictus ; *La Jasante de la Vieille*. *La Jasante* is, roughly, "the prayer," and *la Vieille* is the old mother whose son, a criminal, has been sentenced to death and executed. She comes to weep, to recall the past, and soliloquize above his grave. But what does she recall ? Things of the remotest past ; the first years, the first steps of her child ; and she contrasts these images with those, horrible and recent, which she dare not face.

Think, Louis, long ago, when you were small,
Who would have thought—who could have guessed at all
That you, one day, would come to such an end !
And who'd have thought to see me coming here ?
When you were small you were so sweet and dear !

She does well to recall the past if the pictures of today confront her ; though the world believes in them, and though society has pronounced its verdict, she, his mother, knows very well that the images of the past are true also ; and she cannot consent to part

THE GIFT OF CHILDHOOD

with them. When all is said, they are the truer pictures ; and if there is any inconsistency she will reject the others.

> It isn't true, O say it isn't true,
> All that they said in court ? It wasn't you ?
> And all they wrote about you in the press,
> 'Twas surely just a pack of lies, no less ?
> My little one, my pretty one,
> Would never do the things they say he's done !

In this poem, in which Rictus makes the old woman soliloquize, as he elsewhere makes the pauper or the drunkard soliloquize, there is really something of the idea expressed in a different language by Morgan, a concrete presentation, in the style of the old popular laments, in words calculated to haunt our memory. It is the conflict between the external, social truth, which is on the surface, and the deeper, psychological truth. This latter truth coincides with the truth of childhood ; and only those discover it who have the gift of a childlike nature.

V

The New Year is in many countries at once a day of gifts and a day of vows. But have not the gifts the same significance as the vows ? Are they not, as it were, a more palpable repetition of the latter ? In order to understand these rites—for they are rites— we have only to consider tradition, legend, and folk-lore. The New Year gifts recall those, infinitely precious, which the Three Kings, the Three Wise Men, brought from their distant Orient to the divine Child. But these presents offered to the new-born child by powerful and mysterious personages remind us, strangely, in their turn, of the gifts which fairies, in the folk-tales, or magicians, benevolent or malicious, brought to the child in its cradle. These gifts were good or bad qualities of mind and body. They were presented under the form of a magic word, a charm, or let us say, a vow. These gifts of verbal spells appear, on the other hand, to be akin to the influences which astrology confers on the planets of the natal heavens; and in certain tales it is permissible to see in the fairies who bend over the cradle a personification of the stars that presided over the birth of the child. And this inevitably reminds us of the part played by a star in the legend of the Wise Kings, who were supposed to have known the secrets of the starry heavens.

All this folk-lore may seem very remote from our modern world. Yet it has left very active traces in our language—and therefore in our thought. In proof of this I will cite only the figurative sense of the word "gift," which we use to denote the innate aptitudes, the favours, which a beneficent heaven bestows on each of us in his cradle.

The gifts and the vows that we make on the advent of the New Year are also a touching survival of millenary conceptions. When we make them we liken ourselves to the good fairies and the good genies of the folk-tales. When we receive them we are condescending to being regarded as newly-born children. It is in this respect that the old idea is most charming, and no doubt most fruitful. We are enacting, whether or not we know it, the myth of rebirth. We agree to begin again, like the year itself, and again to become "like unto one of these little ones." By entering alternately into the two rôles—by giving and receiving—we are helping one another to take part in this renovating and salutary game.

VI

We have already told the story of the city full of fountains, whose fountains were demolished in order that the motor-cars of those who came to see it might encounter no obstacles. This was the work of tourists who were simpletons. As a matter of fact this story is significant of many paradoxical situations. It depicts, in a crude and somewhat caricatured form, the intimate contradiction which exists, in some degree, in the act of observation.

Is not every act of observation rightly characterized by the saying of Juvenal which we cited in another chapter ?—"*Propter vitam*" . . . By observing we run the risk of modifying some-

THE GIFT OF CHILDHOOD

thing, and often enough we inevitably modify what we are observing, so that observation, although it is the preliminary condition of all knowledge, contains a sort of contradiction in terms. This vitiates in a fundamental manner all our knowledge, and should warn us not to pride ourselves on it unduly.

Every wild countryside, every savage country, when we begin to visit it, loses its character in the same degree. We cannot observe the butterfly in flight; we kill it and pin it down in order to examine it at leisure; but is it still a butterfly? The painter asks you to pose for your portrait, but when you pose are you still yourself? So it is with all things. The presence of the observer modifies the phenomenon which he is observing; as physical science itself has discovered.

In the observation of man by man, which is supposed to be a source of wisdom and prudence, this is even more marked. A great value is set on that school of keen and reciprocal observation, the life of the salon in highly civilized and social periods. But then everyone feels that he is observed, and so he plays a part. If the observer is very skilful, as La Rochefoucauld was, he will detect, almost everywhere, vanity as the prime motive of these actors; but he has seen actors, and not men, and the picture is distorted.

So we must not plume ourselves too greatly on our knowledge of men and things. Let us turn more often upon the world and men the naïve, keen gaze which makes us become children again.

XVII

CONFIDENCE IN MANKIND

I

"IF there is a pure love, exempt from admixture with our other passions, it is the love hidden in the bottom of the heart, of which we ourselves are unaware."

This is one of the maxims by which La Rochefoucauld reconquers our sympathy, if we were tempted, in respect of so many other parts of his drastic work, to refuse it. It is at the same time one of the keys which he discreetly offers to those who wish to understand him. For we need such keys. He is not anxious to be understood by the vulgar; he is too aristocratic in feeling. His misanthropical judgments (is not this true of all misanthropes?) have a certain modesty. But to those more fastidious minds that deserve to understand him he gives the key, he makes the sign. This passage on love is a sign.

Rouchefoucauld, whom we are asked to see as an Alceste who has fled into his desert, whence he contemplates mankind, is, like the other Alceste, not without a heart; which is embittered, if you will, but only because it had, in the beginning, like all hearts that are in the right place, known a fine native spontaneity. Here is its pure, fresh source. He has told us often enough that everything in man is due to self-esteem! It is pleasant to hear him express, in this *pensée*, though he still speaks with all reserve, of an impulse of pure love.

This impulse, he tells us, is pure so long as it is instinctive and unconscious. Human nature, then, cannot at heart be as radically egoistical as he has elsewhere asked us to believe. It is perhaps rather the human understanding that is the origin of sin. It is at the moment when the conscious mind plays its part that the pure impulse, contaminated by reflection and calculation, may begin to serve the ends of interest or vanity.

Even in the pessimistic moralists, and those who are deliberately objective in their descriptions of the human heart, there are these nuclei of freshness, of childhood, if you will, that one may find if one knows where to look for them ; springs in the desert, we called them. One may find them also in Stendhal, who has more than one trait of kinship with La Rochefoucauld. And when Stendhal shows his well-known predilection for that "energy" which for him signifies the native strength of the noble passions, in their pure and fiercely thoroughbred state, unchecked by moral hypocrisy and civilized calculation, we find in this shrewd psychologist a style of a beautiful naïveté, which is in a sense a comment on La Rochefoucauld's passage on a pure love, free from all admixture.

II

Rudolphe Toepffer, who can say nothing without wit, gives us this gratefully immoral advice, which is perhaps maliciously intended to scandalize certain unduly austere citizens of Geneva : "Do not kill all your vanity ; keep enough to live by." This amiable moralist, who was amiable by intention, all the more so because he had encountered so many cantankerous preachers, knew that the best human qualities are not of pure gold ; they are alloys, in which at least a proportion of base metal is mixed with the precious metal, in order perhaps to give it the consistency which it lacks. He was perspicacious enough to see that nothing —or very little—is done out of pure love, pure wisdom, or pure duty. Some other motive has helped. And is it not all the better that it should be so, if in this way, at least, it is possible to accomplish an action of value ?

Toepffer would undoubtedly agree with La Rochefoucauld in thinking that "virtue would not go so far if vanity did not bear it company." But as he has a better character than the author of the *Maximes* this opinion does not incline toward the misanthropic pessimism in which the latter takes refuge.

To be sure, a moralist ought to reflect on little facts of this kind ; the rescuer who has risked his life does not disdain the medal for life-saving ; the hero already covered with wounds consents, if there is still room for them, to be covered with decorations also (and the decorations may even cover the wounds —truly an example of supererogation) : the artist, who is a humble and authentic servitor of beauty, does not disdain to see his name in large block letters on an announcement, and will quarrel with his confrère over a question of precedence. The moralist will take this for granted. He will smile gently at those zealous pedagogues who refuse to allow the child the spur of emulation. One must not ask too much of human nature.

Above all, we ought to reflect on our littleness, and on the danger that the consciousness of our nonentity, if it were too keen, would deprive us of all courage. So a little vanity is needed to help us to mask our inferiority ; without a doubt, the instinct of self-preservation requires it. Here is an occasion for ringing the changes on the two senses of the word "vanity". If all is vain, in the sense of Ecclesiastes, we must have a little vanity in order sometimes to forget the fact, and to continue to play our part. And this leads us to Bergson's saying : "There is a great deal of modesty at the root of vanity."

III

When one is in search of maxims, one always turns to the work of La Rochefoucauld. We are already on our guard against the bitter savour of pessimism that it exhales. We recall that the *Maximes* owed their origin to a fashionable game ; and this we ought never to forget. This game was itself a refinement of the more gratuitous witticisms of *les précieux* and *les précieuses*, and it retains some of their characteristics. This explains a taste for paradox, which, discreet though it is, marks the majority of the *Maximes*, and which we overlook to some extent in judging them. However, if paradox does not restrict itself to amusing us, or scandalizing us, but holds our attention, so that, despite ourselves, we keep on returning to it, this is because it contains a truth. What precisely is the truth of the *Maximes* ? And can we dissociate it from the radical pessimism which it seems to imply ?

La Rochefoucauld himself points the way to a just criticism when he writes : "The vices enter into the composition of the virtues, as poisons enter into the composition of remedies." This maxim also should be retained as a key, for it does not say, as so many others have the appearance of saying, that the virtues *are* disguised vices ; it says a little more and a little less. No one is shocked by the fact that poisons enter into the composition of remedies ; and remedies are not therefore poisons. Or again, one might say that one must take La Rochefoucauld's analyses, in the chemical sense of the word, as applying not to mixtures, but to compounds, in which the elements, on coming into contact, have produced some new substance, which one will not pretend to identify with them because, on analysis, one detects their presence in it.

Better still, in accordance with the disciplines of thought to which we have become accustomed by a more recent science, we might here invoke the notion of evolution. We might then repeat for ourselves La Rochefoucauld's analyses ; but we should have to remember, once for all, that there is no question of identity, but of development. We should speak, with Nietzsche, of the "genealogy of morals" ; we would even admit, with him, that "good actions are bad actions sublimated" ; but this "sublimated" will give the phrase its tone ; it tells us that a transformation, a transmutation, has been effected. In relating the natural history of our virtues we shall no longer be afraid of referring them to origins by no means brilliant ; and far from discouraging us or inclining us to pessimism, this view may uplift us, like any history of a great destiny that sets out from zero ; a river that one follows from its source, a great man born in a cottage, or the Roman people.

IV

If La Rochefoucauld is the cruel and pessimistic moralist, Vauvenargues, on the contrary, is the humane moralist. He too, of course, makes many reflections which are not to the credit of humanity ; but he makes them with less bitterness than melancholy. He has not the air of regarding his discoveries of our naughtiness as personal triumphs.

He writes, for example : "We are dismayed to see that our very misfortunes have been powerless to correct our faults." I would wager that in approaching humanity thus he is a better teacher than La Rochefoucauld, although his thought is less comprehensive, and his style less forcible.

On reading such a reflection as the above we are persuaded, more than by a harsh criticism, to hope that we may not come to deserve such a judgment. Thus warned, we promise ourselves, without undue boasting, to do a little better another time, and at all events to learn a lesson from misfortune. And this refers to public as well as to private misfortunes.

It is the benevolence that strikes me in Vauvenargue's warning, and this is why he seems to me an educative writer ; for no one has ever educated people by flaying them with sarcasm. One may teach them by awakening regrets, but not by crushing one's pupil with the sense of an irremediable indignity. No one ever got results of any value from a child by constantly repeating that he is a waster ; it is only too easy to make him believe it. But are we not all children in this respect ? La Rochefoucauld is forever berating our vanity. It is Vauvenargues again who replies : "Whatever vanity we may be reproached with, we need sometimes to have someone assure us of our merits."

V

M. Boutourline also is full of benevolence for the human species. Nothing is more tiresome, according to him, than to allow oneself to resort to the pessimistic and inhuman philosophy which seeks to console us for the disappointments of life by saying that the majority of human beings are fools. No, human beings are not fools !

M. Boutourline, for his part, professes that he has met very few fools, and if one insists on the point he replies with this charming euphemism : "They are not stupid, they are preoccupied, which is not the same thing."

This euphemism says more than it seems to say. We have already recognized, while modestly following in Pascal's footsteps, that error is not so much an affair of the intelligence as of the will. We believe what we desire, and in that way deceive ourselves. M. Boutourline is not far from Pascal's way of thinking : "One is preoccupied," he says : that is, one's interest is elsewhere. This is why we are so stupid in the region where our interlocutor appeals to us, without finding us at home. We are not fools ; we are absent. This is clearly to be seen in children, who seem stupid in school because one doesn't contrive to interest them in school, whereas in their games they recover an enviable mental liveliness. That very simple observation comprises a complete programme of education, and one is beginning to realize this : "Don't keep on telling the child that he is a fool, but interest him to begin with." Here Alain is in entire agreement with M. Boutourline. "I don't think there are many imbeciles ; to tell the truth, I have never met one. No ; it is rather the case that there are closed, immured minds : I don't in the least want to open my mind to ideas that will cost me money. And the spendthrift, on the other hand, swears to himself that he won't make up his accounts." (V. 70.) Continuing, he tells us how greatly he admires "the wily people who scent an importunate idea at a distance, and are so clever at changing the conversation". There is a great deal of cunning in this simple trick, and cunning is by no means stupidity. These people's minds are closed to certain ideas which naïve common sense takes in immediately : but they have closed their minds *themselves*, and very skilfully. It takes a great deal of disinterestedness to admit the truth. This is where people go wrong.

VI

One might imagine that what M. Boutourline refuses to attribute to human stupidity he would transfer to the credit of malice.

By no means. He gazes about him with benevolence; observing the hearts of his fellow-creatures as benevolently as their minds. Here again Alain is in agreement with M. Boutourline. "There is, I believe," he writes, "no man so bad that he does not gain by being known. This is because men have not the consistency and constancy that the passions presuppose." (V. 68). This is why one cherishes the greatest hatred for people one has never seen, as is evident in the case of political passions. We attribute to the enemy a coherence and logic in evil which are the product of our imagination; often enough a meeting would dispel all such ideas.

It is worthy of remark that M. Boutourline, who follows quite different paths, nevertheless arrives at the point of pleading in favour of man by drawing attention to his lack of logic. M. Boutourline has a liberal brother-in-law, who has profound convictions, which make him a little unsociable. This unsociable fellow reproaches his brother-in-law bitterly for maintaining friendly relations with the Governor-General Kaméef. Now Kaméef is an excellent friend and a man of the subtlest intelligence. "As a functionary," Boutourline ingenuously admits, "I know absolutely nothing about Kaméef, and I may say that we have never exchanged a word relating to his career. If I were still capable of being astonished by contradictions I should be surprised that Constantine should burden himself with the functions of a governor, which make him the supporter of a very imperfect system of government. Is a man to be despised for not refusing to serve an authority which is by no means the standard-bearer of the Golden Age?" No, M. Boutourline refuses to judge, and he concludes with one of his gently philosophical maxims: "You see, my dear sir, it is better to say that the decency of mankind is illogical than to be in a hurry to exclaim that they have none."

When we feel that people are detestable it is because we attribute to them a greater consistency in their ideas than is actually possible. We do not sufficiently reflect on the fact that when we decide that men are bad we complacently, with an equal degree of loyalty and ingenuousness, make an exception in our own

CONFIDENCE IN MANKIND

favour. Perhaps this is because one is more aware of one's own inconsistencies.

"If we took as much pains," says M. Boutourline, "to discover good intentions in other people as we are ready to take in order to credit them with the worst, what fine fellows we should be!"

VII

"If we had no faults we should not derive so much pleasure from observing them in others."

Habemus confitentem, in the ancient language of the law ; the accused has confessed. La Rochefoucauld, who throughout his maxims manifests so much pleasure in exposing human perversity, confesses at last, in this maxim, the source of this pleasure. It is because we find these faults in ourselves that we are so eager to detect them in others ; otherwise, no doubt, we should hardly be able to endure ourselves.

VIII

And, when we feel inclined to abuse our age, let us beware of excepting ourselves. By consenting to recognize in ourselves the virulent nucleus of the same tendencies that we condemn in our contemporaries we shall be on the way to discovering in them the germ of the protest which has found utterance in us. This will only be an affront to our pride ; but at this expense we shall regain some confidence in our species and our period ; which is well worth a sacrifice, even the sacrifice of the bitter and arrogant pleasure of being in the right against the world.

XVIII

AN APOLOGY FOR THE UNRULY

I

THE little girl who used to say goodnight, on going to bed, to each of the familiar objects around her, was following a procedure from which we might very well take a hint. St. Francis of Assissi did not call only the wolf and the dove his brother and sister; he addressed many inanimate objects in this fashion. "Lifeless objects, have you then a soul?" And Milosz, the great Franciscan poet, did not disdain to do the same in his poems. He spoke of "Brother Cloud", of his "Sister the Rose of the ruins", of "Sister Nettle"; on waking he saluted his "Little Brother Day", and before falling asleep he communed with "Grandfather Night."

There is really such a thing as affection for things, for the humble things which are the adornment and the companions of our lives. Do not those who profess it create around them, by their gestures, an atmosphere of warm benevolence that makes life happier? They are distinguished by the respectful manner in which they handle things, taking hold of them as though they wanted to be taken up, and putting them in their right place, in their right posture. Doubtless this respect, this love, are to some extent bound up with the associated images of certain persons. This object is a souvenir of a beloved person; that makes us think with affection of the labour of the artisan who made it. This amounts to saying that one cannot feel this affection indifferently for all things. Articles manufactured in a series, rigid and inhuman, have not the "soul" of which the poets speak, and even during their lifetime they hardly evoke anything more than the rubbish-heap on which it is their fate to die a quick and unlovely death. These objects have nothing good to say to us, for they do not teach us to love things; while the products of peasant arts and crafts, the lovely utensils which have a history, a patience, which are shaped and moulded by human hands, make a spontaneous appeal to our tenderness, our desire to bid them farewell at night, with the heart if not with the lips, for they constitute a world of our own dimensions, with which we feel ourselves in agreement.

II

But perhaps you will say, these unbeautiful objects, manufactured in series, are more practical? Take care! Those who have meditated on beauty are generally in agreement on this point: that those things are beautiful which are perfectly adapted to their ends; a beautiful object is that which has the form of its function. This is what aesthetics teaches us. But we must accept the inference; that the beautiful and the useful should not really be in opposition. If we are shown that some ugly object is more practical, no doubt some term of the equation, some essential imponderable, has been forgotten. If you allow yourself to be convinced you will certainly be defended; and if your sense of the beautiful continues to protest, by all means listen to it as your surest instinct.

You may be sure that the dreary, rationalized dwelling-house of whose perfect comfort you have been assured will prove, when you come to live in it, to be inhuman, with creaking floors and hinges, and will make you regret the peasant's hearth. You may be sure that the vandals who, under spurious and short-sighted pretexts of utility, cut down beautiful old trees and tear up delightful hedges, and do their utmost to transform a noble countryside into a dismal suburb, are not in the long run promoting the true well-being of their neighbourhood. If we question ourselves sincerely we shall see that this holds good of estates, costumes, utensils, and furniture; we do not always see where the shoe pinches; we do not always perceive the relation between our discomfort and the beauty lightly sacrificed on the vulgar altar of utility; we shall perhaps be reluctant to recognize that we are justly punished for our sacrilege. But we discover with astonishment, in the course of time, that this rationalized and practical world which has been made for us is decidedly less pleasant to live in than the other. We are simply not so happy in it. What we are told is practical, and is not beautiful, ought to be regarded with suspicion. The safest course is to escape from it as quickly as possible.

III

We are much less given than of old to correcting children, though they sometimes need correction ; but we have taken it into our heads to correct our brooks and streams, which are unable to protest.

Pleasant, playful, mischievous brooks, they are on the whole very charming and very innocent. Perhaps, in a fit of seasonal petulance, they sometimes overflow a little into the adjacent meadows. Within the memory of our ancestors they have never done any serious harm, and it is admitted that even their passing fits of anger were among the incidents that introduce a pleasant and unexpected variety into the monotony of our days. Was it really so useful an undertaking to correct them, as people have begun to do, with a zeal worthy of La Fontaine's pedants, and a euphemism whose irony no one is willing to perceive ? Once more we might return to the problem of the good and the beautiful : That which offends against beauty is in all probability not really useful ; this is a rule that should never be overlooked. However, we have made our inquiry ; we have been given the local details which have, under the circumstances, largely justified our supposition ; sometimes the interested persons, the first to be consulted, had grave doubts of the advantage to be obtained.

However, our brooks are now securely piped underground or turned into dreary rectilinear canals ; once more a charming piece of the countryside has been spoilt. The worst of it is that the example is followed, and at the present rate of progress all our

AN APOLOGY FOR THE UNRULY

brooks, the most limpid and the most well-behaved, are in danger of being so dealt with unless something is done about it.

"Do they ever reflect," one of the interested parties said to me—although he was an engineer—"do they ever reflect what a pleasure it was for the children to play with this pleasant companion, whose temperament was like their own—this brook —and to learn from it all sorts of interesting things about the habits of all sorts of picturesque creatures ?" But the brook is rectified. A pretty kind of pedagogy, this ! People are doing their utmost to make the world a boring place. And a child who is bored begins to behave stupidly. So one must set to work and thoroughly correct the children ? Would it not have been better to rectify the brooks a little less ?

IV

The rectification of brooks : this is only one example ; for human ingenuity seems to be exerting itself, in our days, with abundant help from science, and with much success, to create fresh causes of boredom. Telephone posts, dismal factories, the slag-heaps outside workshops, dumps, barbarous, dull industrial cities, leprous suburbs, proliferating, heartbreaking . . . Do we sufficiently reflect that all these delightful things are specifically modern ? and if one is to judge the tree by the fruit, what are we to think of the mind that is responsible for such products ? Perhaps we ought to say by-products. But they are very pervasive. And does not everything that is vexatious bear a mark of infamy that should condemn it without appeal ? They have even made work vexatious and boring, which is really unbelievable. "Only look !" a distinguished psychologist said to me but lately : "look at the faces of the people sitting in a row in the train a little before eight o'clock in the morning, in winter, in a great city ; it is an ominous spectacle !" Why this boredom, oozing out on every hand in the world that man has made for himself with such ability ?

Perhaps the question can be answered in a word : it is *artificial*.

We are asked to make gestures which obey no pre-existing instincts of our nature; we are offered spectacles to which nothing within us responds. All these things are technically perfect, but they are no less perfect in their disregard of the laws of life. And this is where the matter becomes serious; the man who is bored, no less than the child, begins to behave foolishly. The complaint is made that our contemporaries have often only rather miserable distractions; but that would be of no great importance. What we know only too well is that they will end by smashing everything; after the fashion of children afflicted with boredom.

Yet there is one remedy for boredom, a sovereign and simple remedy; beauty. Artists do not know what it is to be bored. Whatever you have to do, never be content with being a technician; be an artist; above all be an artist; seek beauty in the first place, and the rest will be added unto you.

V

We were speaking of the energy and inconscience with which our contemporaries are ransacking Nature. An acquaintance, a sensible inhabitant of this countryside, who loves it, drew my attention to a fresh depredation which had just been committed. "It was done in a turn of the hand," he said. "This place, which yesterday was one of the most charming spots in the canton, is today as shabby and dismal as if a wave of destruction had swept over it. Yes, you might really say that they are jealous because they have not had the war and its devastation; you would wager that they too want their little devastations, so they perpetrate them for themselves." I tried to pacify my friend, for I could see that he was very angry; but in my heart I felt that he was not far wrong. He continued: "This murder was perpetrated like all murders, stealthily, without warning. One knew nothing about it—and then the thing was done. And look you, in the town things were going the same way recently, with the destruction of buildings and of fine urban sites. When one realized what was happening it was always too late; one was faced with the

AN APOLOGY FOR THE UNRULY

accomplished fact, and the jeering laughter of the vulgar. But an association has been formed of citizens who love their city ; they call themselves 'the Watch'. They have undertaken to be on the look-out ; to know what is being said, what is cooking in the pot of these demolishers. The Watch, it seems, has already saved quite a number of fine things."

"Then," I said, "it's a sort of local guard ?"

"You have said it ; a local guard of beautiful things. And it is high time, at the rate things are going, that we had these local guards in our villages. There are, I know, societies for the protection of Nature, but they fly too high ; they don't see what is happening in detail, and that is what matters. Local guards were levied for the defence of the country. Well, the defence of our copses, our brooks, our shady lanes, our hedges, with their birds, of all this beauty by which we live, ingrates that we are—this also is the defence of the country ! Yes, a local guard. Or better still, francs-tireurs !" And he jumped into his train.

VI

People talk a great deal about the organization of leisure. Here and there, indeed, there has been a fair amount of such organization. This is an undertaking that has its proselytes, its enthusiasts, its fanatics. It is lauded as a sign of decisive progress ; as the prodrome of a new age. It is progress, certainly, if we note what people commonly do with their leisure, and how they manage to waste it. But let us always have a care when we record this too evident progress. True progress would start from a good to proceed to a greater good ; but when one starts from an evil one should speak not of progress, but of a remedy, of separation, or patching up ; which, after all, is only an advance toward a lesser evil. And this, it seems to me, applies to the greater part of the progress in labour legislation during the past hundred years ; it consisted, very often, only of the introduction of the means of diminishing great endemic evils recently introduced by the industrial revolution. It was better than doing nothing ; but we have no reason to be proud of ourselves and to speak so loudly of progress.

And is it not the same with the organization of leisure ? Let us say, rather, it is another aspect of the same tragedy. Men whose living conditions have been disorganized by the workshop, by machinery, by the octopus-like city, have been torn away from their true nature, and have lost the health of their instincts. It is for this reason that at the times when they find themselves suddenly at liberty they begin to behave foolishly. They must learn over again the saner gestures which their instincts ought to dictate to them. This is why their leisure ought to be organized.

But in the coupling of these two words is there not something that grates, that ought to arouse our attention ? Is not this remedy rather disquieting, as a symptom ? Ask advice of the Flemish peasants gathered together in the *kermesses* of the Flemish painters, of those who are celebrating the day of the Three Kings in Jordaens' picture, of the musicians and the women so harmoniously grouped in the "Concert" of Giorgione. Ask our good Rabelais for his advice. Here you will be greeted with a roar of laughter, and the curé of Meudon will send you, for further information, to the Abbey of Thélème, on whose great gateway he has inscribed the memorable words : *"Fais ce que vouldras."*

VII

People now speak only of the team spirit. They assure us that the team spirit in sport is the first apprenticeship to the social spirit which ought to reign throughout the community. That is all very well ; but human infirmity is such that in every truth there is a germ of error, as soon as one becomes enamoured of it. Do you not think that we have almost reached that stage with our team spirit ?

Our epoch has seen, rising on almost every hand, these massive, coherent, organized groups, which demand and obtain from their members an absolute devotion, which is a fine thing. Are they not in this respect like large teams ? But when they exceed

AN APOLOGY FOR THE UNRULY

certain quantitative limits they begin to make us uneasy, to alarm us ; we are ready to say that they are assuming the appearance of monsters, and that this fine devotion is so blind that it is becoming a danger, for it is dangerous to be blind, and still more dangerous to be a great blind monster with a thousand heads, a monster blind with a thousandfold blindness. Is not this calculated to damp our enthusiasm ?

I am afraid the team, when all is said, may be constituted only at the cost of a certain sacrifice of the critical spirit, and the larger the team the more complete must be the sacrifice. This is when the danger becomes apparent. And it leads one to ask oneself whether the unreserved exaltation of the critical spirit does not proceed from the current prejudice which overvalues action at the expense of thought. The team is necessary for action ; it is the convergence of forces for the maximum effect. But thought follows other paths. It is free and voluntary. It has a recalcitrant air. It puts everything to the question. A certain great worthy said : "I think, therefore I am." He did not say "We are." He was hardly thinking of teams. He kept to his own clique. A good thinker has to begin by being a rebellious thinker. Now, we are greatly in need of good thinkers. I would wager that we have more need of them than of well-behaved teams. And we also need unruly, rebellious thinkers.

IX

When anyone wishes to give us the lofty notion of the ancient Egyptian civilization that we ought very properly to entertain, he never fails to call attention, amongst other relics, to the wall-painting in which some divinity of the world beyond the tomb is seen weighing souls on a practicable pair of scales ; and this does in fact point to a highly evolved conception of morality. Taking a few giant strides across countries and centuries, we find the Scales, the Balance again on the emblazoned fountains of our mediaeval cities ; it is seen in the hands of an allegorical Justice ; whether Justice is terrestial or spiritual, the same image appears, and impresses itself on the imagination. I am almost inclined to say that the Balance is essentially the emblem of civilization.

This is even truer than it seems at the first glance. For does not all civilization presuppose a slow conquest of thought, an emergence of thought, as in Rodin's block of marble ? Now what does the French word for thought, *pensée*, really mean ? Where does it come from ? It is the same word as *pesée*, weighing. Originally it means weighing and nothing else. There is thought, *pensée*, as soon as we understand how to balance the scales, as soon as we are able to emerge from our own standpoint and to adopt that of another person ; which is the only thing that enables us, as we say today, to be objective, more or less. It would be simpler to say that it enables us to be just. Thought is at work as soon as we are able to weigh the pros and cons, as soon as we are capable of awaiting with patience and minute attention the unstable and sensitive immobility of the beam. For that matter, is not the essential act of thought known as judgment ? And this leads us by another path to justice.

In the domain of action, as soon as the prudent wisdom of justice gives way to the régime of summary executions without judgment ; in the domain of thought, as soon as critical discussion is replaced by the slogan of the team, the world moves a step towards barbarism. *To suspend our judgment* is, according to Descartes, one of the first principles of thought; it is also one of the first principles of civilization. We ought really to imagine ourselves as suspending our judgment as the light and sensitive beam of a balance is suspended.

X

The festival of youth has had a great success in the village. Do not let us complain of the societies and groups which are seen emerging on every hand. Still, I think it is well that the group should not express the mere instinct of the herd animal. Elective affinities must play a part, and the members should be grouped around some flag or standard.

AN APOLOGY FOR THE UNRULY

I can understand a gymnastic society, a musical society, a salon in which there is conversation. But to assemble simply because one is a member of the nation's "youth"—is that altogether justified? Why, then, don't we have an association of men six feet in height, or a confraternity of the red-haired? Youth is a fine thing, so is health, and so is intoxication. There is also a communicative warmth that irradiates itself, round the cabaret table, among those who drink together. Do not let us blame them too severely! There is always something dynamic in human warmth, but it is dangerous also when it is only heat. And when young people are together this warmth is generated; and it stimulates the blood in a certain manner. But does the warmth go much further than the blood? When all is said, a group which unites round the same interest people of all ages is an act of civilization, but a group which is based only on the heat of the blood is animal in character.

When I was learning French I was taught that the adjective *jeune*, young, is employed as a substantive only in speaking of animals. One says: the cat has had young. But in speaking of human beings one says: young people, young girls, young athletes. The new jargon, that speaks of *les jeunes*, "the young", gives me an uneasy feeling. I cannot help thinking of the offspring of the cat—or the wolf. There is something animal and primitive in the term.

To "march together" is good; but one ought to know why one is marching.

XIX

WITHDRAWAL INTO ONE'S TENT

It is not only the thinker and the critic who does well to hold himself apart from the team. It may be that the man of action, and action of the most authentic kind, is also rebellious and unruly ; and this will not in any way detract from his action ; far from that, it is in this way that he obeys the rhythm of the fiery and ungovernable nature that makes him the man of action that he is. Now, a man never gives to the utmost of his capacity unless he is allowed to act in accordance with his own rhythm and the truth of his own nature. Does he withdraw himself at the moment when the team counts upon him and appeals to him ? Let him withdraw. His hour will come, and when he emerges from his lair he will leap like a lion. There is a very old and very fine story to this effect. You remember that the *Iliad* does not celebrate so much the "Trojan war", as people are always repeating, as "the Wrath of Achilles"; Achilles sulking, Achilles keeping to his own clique, and retiring into his tent. The other chieftains are distressed and full of deference ; they implore him, they politely adjure him to return ; in which they show themselves shrewder than our modern teams. Today it is clear that Achilles would have been regarded as a deserter and executed—which is really not at all Hellenic. Homer's beings belonged to a society wiser than our societies of teams and groups. They are sensible of greatness ; they know where it resides, they know that it is in Achilles, and that it is with him in his tent. They are full of respect for this tent and what it contains. Their great orators negotiate. Who was it who decided that speech is contemptible ? They lose nothing by waiting. They know very well that they are losing nothing. One day what is happening will strike at Achilles where he is still vulnerable—at his heart. Then he will

146

emerge from his tent like a rising sun, like a young and terrible god. And he will carry off the victory.

The Right to Withdrawal

"To assert his rights to retirement." This expression is full of irony ; all the more so when there is another retreat than that of old age and fatigue, a more essential retirement, though one hardly thinks of asserting one's rights to it. We have suggested that our modern society would not have allowed Achilles to retire into his tent. But there are other types of faithful retirement to which our society shows itself hardly more amenable. It is by no means certain that it would have allowed John the Baptist to retire into the desert. The Middle Ages conceived the admirable retreat of the cloister, where those who wished to tear themselves away from the tumult of the world and the barbarism of battle found an asylum ; but the modern epoch has conceived the notion of mobilizing the monks ; barbarism has become totalitarian. Our society would look with disapproval on the anchorites who would ask of it nothing but a cave ; it would invite them first of all to present themselves before a board which would issue permits of occupation, and one can imagine how they would be received ; it would offer them, in the place of a cave, a padded cell ; it would simply regard them as madmen. Or let us rather say that it would make madmen of them ; it *makes* lunatics. For there is nothing that will drive a man to lunacy like the claim to a form of existence which is not recognized by the society in which he is living. When we study certain originals, as one calls them, certain bizarre, shy, and unbalanced personages, we see that these were richly endowed natures, but solitaries, who had suffered from a world which did not recognize their right to solitude and withdrawal. This refusal on the part of the group develops in the individual a sense of inferiority and guilt that gnaws at him like a cancer. To restore such beings to a happy equilibrium it is often enough to approve their secret vocation and to incite them with a *clear conscience* to live in accordance with their nature.

Other societies, thereby giving proof of a higher intelligence, have accepted and integrated the vocations of these solitaries. In India they are highly respected ; and accordingly they develop all the fruits of their vocation.

We still had our beggars and vagabonds, a loose and tacit confraternity, into which authentic solitaries, full of prayer and meditation, could enter surreptitiously by means of their mask of poverty. But our societies, with their team spirit and their sanitary services, were quick to sweep away such ordure. Shining with cleanliness and hypocrisy, our societies consider the condition of mendicant to be unworthy of human dignity, for which, under certain circumstances, they display a surprising zeal. What voice could tell them with a sufficient emphasis that their lips are dripping with lies ? Who will dare to ask them, face to face, whether human dignity is not often far more affronted by the circumstances of the clerk, the driver of a refuse-tank, or the worker at the moving bench, than by those of the tramp or the street singer ? I see more just pride in many a mendicant than in many of our well-paid slaves. The condition of beggar used to be the last refuge of certain indomitable characters. The society that has no beggars left fills me with anxiety. I know of one perfect country, a clean country. "You see," they told me with all the satisfaction of a good conscience and mediocrity, "you see, we have no more beggars !" But I knew the last beggar in that country ; he threw himself into the river.

XX

VERLAINE

Le Poéte Maudit.

I

We may recall the quip or precept of Verlaine: "Take eloquence and wring its neck". But we say that eloquence is a social quality, and that if poetry, at this moment of its history, divorces eloquence it is divorcing itself from the community. This rupture is pathetic; its symptoms are multiple and varied. There was the exile of Hugo; the withdrawal of Lamartine, who wrote, during his retreat, "The truth is that I am dying of chagrin." There were the cases of Flaubert and Baudelaire, prosecuted for offences against public morality. Lastly, there are the "accursed poets"; above all, there is Verlaine, whose rupture with society was perhaps the most conspicuous, and who paraded through the repudiated city like an aggressive and churlish symbol. It is worth our while to study in him, and through him, the tragedy that outlives him, the tragedy of an epoch, which is not yet concluded.

II

It was Verlaine who introduced the notion, destined to become famous, of the "accursed poets", by assembling under this title some articles on misunderstood and unfortunate poets—among whom was the "poor Lélian" in person, and also Rimbaud, "self-accurst". But the idea was already present in the *Poèmes saturniens*, where it appeared under the banner of *Les Grotesques* (which links up with Théophile Gautier's book on the famous originals of the 17th century):

> Their legs the steeds that bear their weight,
> Their gaze the only gold they know,
> Along the path of random feet,
> Haggard and tattered, on they go.
>
> And plucking at a shrill guitar
> With hands that never knew constraint
> They snuffle many a bizarre,
> Nostalgic and rebellious plaint . . .

As for the *Poètes maudits*, if they are responsible for any philosophy it is that of Vigny's *Stello* : "Republican of every bonnet or monarchist of every stamp, or indifferent to what you will of the public life, is it not true that *et nunc et semper et in saecula* the sincere poet sees and feels himself to be *cursed* by the rule of every interest, O Stello ?" (III). And in *Mes Hôpitaux* there are pages on Hégésippe Moreau—who died in hospital—which might form yet another chapter of the *Poètes maudits* : "As for his death in hospital, allow me to deplore it no more than is proper . . . society, under whatever régime—read *Stello* !—does not exist in order to glorify the poets . . ." (*Chroniques de l'Hôpital*, I). But here there is some optical illusion. It is not true that the poet feels that he is always accurst. At the present juncture of history, yes, he perceives that he is out of favour.

III

Since we have come to the hospital, let us remain there for a moment. We may be sure of finding Verlaine there in one of his more Lélian-like incarnations. It is true that we might equally well have looked for him in prison ; the prison of which he writes in *Amour* :

> Cells ! Humanitarian prisons ! Keep it hid,
> Your pointless horror, the progress of hypocrites !

The hospital, reformed by progress, is like the prison. Verlaine speaks of "the doctors and students, rather sceptical and con-

VERLAINE

ceited" : the patients "do not seem to be overjoyed by the departure of the Sisters". (*Mes Hôpitaux*, I) ; the students are "vulgar poseurs . . . inhuman, absolutely insolent" (ibid, IV). Lastly, while wishing to be just and grateful where gratitude is due, he cannot refrain from fulminating against "the atrocious idea . . . of the modern hospital for the modern poet, who can . . . only find it black as death and the tomb . . . black as the absence of charity, your modern hospital, thoroughly civilized as you have made it, men of this century of money and filth and sputum." (*Chronique de l'Hôpital*, II.)

You hear how the epithets "modern" and "civilized" are beginning to sound like slaps in the face. "The absence of charity" is the defect. But where have we already come across a diatribe against hospitals, by one speaking in the name of charity, a wholly personal virtue ? You may remember that it was in Pascal. One is surprised to find these two men of genius, so different at every point, agreeing in the condemnation of eloquence. But here, in respect of hospitals, is another unexpected agreement ; and we begin to wonder whether these two cases of agreement do not proceed from similar impulses. Pascal and Verlaine had one thing in common—this distrust of the forum and the crowd. (Pascal writes his *Lettres* to "*one* Provincial of his acquaintance". They have in common, too, a reflex of withdrawal from institutions, a common passion for the human being, who is necessarily in the singular. "I have shed such a drop of blood for thee," says Pascal's God. "What, I, I, to be able to love You !" says Verlaine to his God. Is their wrath against eloquence really anything else than the expression, in each, of a similar quest for personal intimacy ? But the community, the State, knows nothing of persons. And does not the modern State ignore them more than any ?

IV

Thus, by arraigning the hospital, we come to arraign modernity. It is above all—would one have believed it ? in the book *Amour* that Verlaine discharges his bile with the most violent, the most partial, and often the most unjust enthusiasm.

He attacks, to begin with, the particular type of modern man known as the bourgeois, in which he might be no more than a romantic, an "artist", or a Bohemian. But he already speaks with another accent when he accuses "bourgeois spite" of blackening his name (*A Emile Blémont*), where he pokes fun at the indignant outcries of "Madame Prudhomme" (*Lucien Létinois*, XV). The bourgeois is not only ridiculous, he is odious ; and the declaration of war assumes a frankly revolutionary tone, as in the *Ballade en l'Honneur de Louise Michel*.

> Citoyenne ! votre evangile
> On meurt pour ! c'est l'Honneur ! et bien
> Loin des Taxil et des Bazile,
> Louise Michel est très bien.

In addition to the bourgeois, he extends a more general criticism to "this stupid age" (*Un conte*), in which he is condemned to drag his idiotic, arthritic leg after him ; and he rails at "the shameful hour" when the prophet that he is feels himself "dying of the times in which we are living" . . . while "abysmal disasters yawn beneath us (*Saint Graal*) ; he denounces *A propos d'un centenaire de Calderon* this "impious and ridiculous century". He does not mince his words when he speaks of the progressive, republican, and humanitarian ideologies, which he regards as so much nonsense. It is even painful to see him, now and again, falling into step behind the most dubious and venomous—and most bourgeois !—slogans of the reactionary party of the day ; by which we see that he has not the hard, sensible head of a Péguy, and that his brain (the brain of an alcoholic, it must be confessed) is sometimes disappointingly unstable and open to influence ; but when it is his heart that speaks he goes straight to the point, he sees clearly and accuses justly. The sonnet to *Louis II de Bavière*, the mad knight, seems to echo the noble despair of an unrealizable ideal :

> Only true king of our century, I salute thee !

VERLAINE

And the statuette which he erects to the Bavarian and Wagnerian Hamlet has all the majesty of a symbol.

What he appreciated above all in the Church was that it also showed itself to be unshakable. What he asked of it was that it should be the refuge and the breakwater against the tide of the century.

How good the Church is in this age of hatred !
(Saint-Benoit Joseph Labre.)
Blessed art thou, O Lord, who madest me a Christian
In these times of ferocious ignorance and hatred.
(Paraboles.)

And two of the poems in this collection are dedicated—which makes them even more significant—one to Léon Bloy, the master of invective, and the other to Huysmans, the same who was one day to astonish the world by his resounding cry : *A rebours !*[1] denouncing with a fine fanaticism the modern error, which has been evolving in accordance with its inner logic since the initial *faux pas* of the Renaissance ; arguing that we ought to turn back and actually retrace our steps to the Middle Ages and their "cathedral". And this cry Verlaine made his own in *Sagesse*, when, not content with reverting to the "wisdom of a Louis Racine", he sought to sail beyond the "Gallican and Jansenist" 17th century to the

Middle Age, so delicate, so vast,
Upon thy wings of stone, O mad Cathedral ! (X).

Yes, the Cathedral was mad ; neither more nor less than the King of Bavaria with the madness of the Cross.

V

This break with an epoch, with a class, with a society, could not be effected, above all in a being as spontaneous as Verlaine, without manifesting itself in the poet's bearing and his dress. The repudiation of the modern bourgeois is followed by the repudiation of the bourgeois fashion, which, in the first place, is unpardonably ugly. Every artist repudiates it instinctively, or

[1] Which may mean either *Back !* or *The Wrong Way*. (Tr.)

submits to it only under protest. In the 19th century he was subject to two opposing temptations; dandyism and the extreme of shabbinesss. The two temptations were mutually opposed, yet they were closer to each other than might appear. Beggarliness displays in its own fashion the intimate elegance which is nauseated by the bourgeois smartness of the mannequin in the shop window—true elegance despises elegance. And it is so true that dandyism and seediness can co-exist in the same individual, as we see from the example of Maurice du Plessys, the type of the perfect "decadent". Here at all events is what Lucien Aressy writes of him in his pictureque volume on the *Dernière Bohème; Verlaine et son milieu.*[1] "Imagine a dandy whose clothes are in rags, but who has pinned them together so well that the whole is decent. The influence of Verlaine was perceptible in this costume, which might have been that of a Verlaine covered with dust." (p. 128.) A, Baudelaire, as Oscar Wilde set the fashion in dandyism, Verlaine, for his part, preferred seediness. On the whole, this reaction is probably saner and more human. Not that the author of the *Fêtes Galantes* had not felt the attraction and the nostalgia of the erudite elegancies of yesteryear!

> Des messieurs bien mis
> Sans nul doute amis
> Des Royers-Collards,
> Vont vers le château,
> J'estimerais beau
> D'êtres ces vieillards.

But they are ancients of another day, a little quaint, a little spectral. If they cannot be incorporated in the present it is better to be frankly a tatterdemalion.

And a Verlaine proclaims and displays his seediness.

> Je vais gueux comme un rat d'église.
> (*Chanson pour Elle*, II.)

"I go about (as we might say) as seedy as a church mouse."

[1] Jouve, Paris, 1923.

VERLAINE

> Que me fait que le temps soit sombre
> S'il fait soleil en moi, chez toi
>   Et que le plaisir pie
>   A notre gueuserie.
> (Ibid, XVI.)

> "What do I care that the weather's poor
> If the sun is in me when I enter your door !
>   If only pleasure smile
>   Upon our rags awhile ?"

As for dandyism, if he had known its temptation he had long ago left it behind him as he hobbled along with his heavy walking-stick :

> Ah ! j'en suis revenu des "dandysmes cruels"
> Vrais ou faux, dans la vie (accident ou coutume)
> Ou dans l'art, ou tout bêtement dans la costume.[1]
> (Bonheur, XVIII.)

Rather a hundred times be a tatterdemalion ! At this rate, at least, one could still rub elbows with the people, and feel oneself one among these worthy folk, whom the newspapers, it is true, and "instruction" have rendered passably stupid, though they retain, nevertheless

> Quelque saveur encor de parole et d'idée . . .
> Même je les préfère aux mufles de ma sphère.[2]
> (Ibid, X.)

VI

Seediness is the visible aspect of the "poète maudit". It expresses, neither more nor less than the repudiation of eloquence and the taste for *argot*, the poet's divorce from society. But this beggarly Verlaine knows very well why he is divorced—he knows that society is shaking him off. He knows very well why he

---

[1] I have lost my infatuation for the "cruel dandyisms", true or false, accidents or habitual, whether in art or quite unintelligently in dress.
[2] Still some pungency of speech and thought . . .
I even prefer them to the rotters of my world.

adopts, "as though it were a lofty defiance, the banner of the decadents, on which he chooses to see displayed all the violent splendours of the Byzantine Empire."[1] No, it is hardly for him to intone the official litanies of progress ! In 1889, the very year of the Exposition and the Eiffel Tower, he preferred to write to Cazals—from Aix-les-Bains—regarding the hero of Villiers de l'Isle-Adam's *l'Eve future* : "This hero is a miracle of Symbolism : modern science ending in a stupendous catastrophe ; *literally the death of a soul* . . . Read it again : (Letter of 26th August, 1889).[2] For us, who know the historical sequel, this is not so badly perceived, nor said. The beggar, by going outside the community, retires far enough to see clearly. He is no longer one of those who are deluded by eloquence. And he knows to which side he should turn in order to touch the true values :

Douceur et charité, seule toute-puissance.
(*Bonheur*, XXII.)

[1] Cited by Aressy, *Op. cit.*, p. 31.
[2] *Ibid.*, p. 82.

XXI

ART AND THE EPOCH

I

THERE are, for a work of art, two recipes for immediate success ; it must resemble everything, or it must resemble nothing. It must be in the fashion or it must shock the beholder.

In order to succeed, an artist willingly offers sacrifices either to the power of shocking the public, or to the fashion ; in either case he is sacrificing to stupidity. These are equivalent tactics, and closer to each other than would appear. How is it that some artists are able to pass from one to the other with the completest ease ? (And are there not also shocking fashions ?)

The purest artist has recourse to neither tactics. He astonishes without jarring the nerves, and thus he does not at once attract attention.

II

On the one hand are the pontiffs, on the other the buffoons.

The pontiffs are the profiteers of art. Theirs is age, and money. They are wealthy and decorated. Decoration and decorum are theirs. They are decorated with all the orders, and above all with the decorations for order ; moral order, social order : they are ornamental. Deliberately religious as a matter of decency, conservatives as a matter of decorum. They are representative men—they represent in the intransitive sense of the word. This is to say that they do not represent this or that ; they are just representative. In short, decoration and representation. Perfect decorations for every kind of representation.

The buffoons are young, or try to seem so. Or rather, they are spurious youngsters. They play pranks. They try to be droll ;

sometimes they are, but they soon begin to bore us; buffoonery is monstrous. The others were the salesmen in the temple. These are the mountebanks of the fair held in the market-place—which is the forecourt of the temple. They want to startle and amaze the public. They are exhibitionists.

But extremes meet. The buffoons are the buskers gesticulating on the stage which the pontiffs decorate with their faded tones. They are in good company. The pontiffs have arrived, the buffoons are the *arrivistes*. When a buffoon arrives he becomes a pontiff. The buffoons are the pick of the candidates for the pontificate. In the meantime they treat as pontiffs all who are not buffoons, while the pontiffs treat as buffoons all who are not pontiffs.

The pontiffs have the avowed pedants on their side; the buffoons have the snobs, and also all the pedants who are terrified of appearing pedants (which today amounts to saying, nearly all the pedants). A few artists even may allow themselves to be captured, for the buffoon is still an artist in his category; he has a family resemblance; all the more so as every true artist must at least once in his life have felt an impulse to play the buffoon, an itch to flabbergast all the people one meets whose faces need slapping. There are also some true artists who have lost their way among the buffoons; and there are some who make grimaces in order to earn their living (like the weeping Pierrot). And this leads to confusion. There are also some true artists who pontificate; for in the artist there is something of the priest and the pride of the priest. And the priest turns to the pontiff as pride to vanity.

One could name some great artists who, by certain of their gestures, have been members of one of these two categories—sometimes of both. The young romantics played the buffoon pleasantly enough. The aged Hugo pontificates, not without real majesty. There is something of the tragic buffoon in Baudelaire. We see that where there is true greatness its effigy bears the marks of both pontification and buffoonery, but it by no means depends on these mannerisms for its existence, and gains by dispensing with them.

Art has to live among the pontiffs and the buffoons. All periods have been well provided with pontiffs. None has had so many buffoons as ours; with the result that the latter are today the most dangerous enemies of art. The artist educated by the examples of the past is determined not to be a pontiff. Perhaps tomorrow he will be now determined not to be a buffoon.

Come, then! Forward! Between GAGA and DADA, between this Charybdis and Scylla, steer a straight course!

III

THE CONVERSION OF THE PROFESSORS.

The professors were, from remotest antiquity, on the side of the pontiffs; have you noticed that today they are going over, with arms and baggage, to the side of the buffoons? They have been made to feel so ashamed of being old and bearded academicians! So they could think of nothing better than to rush to the other extreme. Moreover, should not one always be objective, scientific, examining all phenomena? And what phenomena are the buffoons! The professors of today swear by science and objectivity as those of yesterday swore by Aristotle and the rules of art. The result of the whole conjuncture is surprising enough; no one marches more briskly, with a more convinced air, than the professors, in robes or without, behind the trumpeters of the latest fad. But once more, they are not in the movement. Their intelligence—epimethean and by no means promethean, as Spitteler would say—their intelligence, apt enough at classification, is incurably deficient in the antennae that make discoveries. Their good will is extremely maleficent; no one has done more than they have done toward maintaining the new fads, by conferring patents of nobility upon them and giving them an imposing appearance of seriousness.

THE MYTH OF MODERNITY

IV

To be up to date—to be of one's time ! We hear this password everywhere. But let us call things by their names. To be of one's time, to be up to date ; I would wager that nine times out of ten this means merely : to be in the fashion.

V

Liberty is an arduous task. Those who have broken away from a dogmatic ideology seem exhausted by the effort, and relapse with disconcerting facility into superstition. So and so has just left his church or chapel, banging the door behind him, and now he swallows the first preposterous tale of table-turning. Some are capable of understanding that there is nothing glorious about being a native of one's country, but are all the more frantically anxious to be men of their time, which is not a matter of any great merit. Their time, their unfortunate time ! Yet another village belfry in four-dimensional space !

VI

Here is a pretty paradox to unravel : In Einstein's time, the time when time is conjured away, how can one be of one's time save by being out of time ?

VII

To be of one's country ? To be of one's time ? Of course one is the one and the other, as naturally as one breathes. But to make a profession of it ? Great men do not behave thus. I remember what Spitteler once wrote to me : "I have never been a Swiss poet, nor a German poet, but a European poet—internatial (sic) and intertemporal. It is a mere accident of birth that I have had to make use of the German language." Genius has such a sense of being *elsewhere* !

VIII

You who are afraid of not being in the fashion, reassure yourself and go your way. In our days fashion runs so quickly through its cycle that it will end, sooner or later, by coinciding with you. To be a little behind the fashion is the surest way of being in advance of the fashion.

IX

Under so many circumstances one sees the contrast between hasty strength that spends its capital in small change and is equivalent to weakness, and restrained strength which accumulates and patiently waits.

This contrast emerges between two different manners of "being of one's time". There is the journalistic fashion of the feeble and the vulgar who want everything of "the very latest", of those who obediently follow the seesaw motion of the changing wind, of the wind that carries now hither, now thither, the unchanging slogans : Novelty ! Actuality ! And there is the fashion of the strong, of those who are able to be of their time but to stand away from it, thereby grasping its perspective. These are not merely of their time : they make their time, which is better. They are "above the hurly-burly", but is it not obvious that this very remoteness affords them the surveying gaze of the leader ? Is there any presence more convincing than that of the *inactuate considerations* ?

X

OF OUT AND OUT EVOLUTIONISM, OR THE ANXIETY TO CATCH THE LAST BOAT.

The classic artists considered that art should strive toward an unchanging model of perfection, and each, for his own part, endeavoured to approach this model.

If we could only do so as well as the ancients ! The modern thinkers have changed all that ; they have conceived the idea of evolution.

The idea of evolution is one of the most beautiful and most dangerous ideas, one of those which is most subject to abuse, which is most liable to be falsely applied, as soon as we apply it to anything other than the transformations of living species; in respect of which it achieved its first success. The Greek author Nicolaë has called attention to the false social Darwinism which perpetrates the nonsense of assimilating the wars of the peoples to the "struggle for existence" of the species, and seeks to justify the former by the latter. The British author MacDougall has forcibly denounced the fallacy which identifies human progress (the wholly external improvement of technique) with the natural evolution of living forms. But people still continue to talk nonsense.

Since Brunetière introduced into literary criticism the idea of the "evolution of styles" the artists have never stopped talking of "movements", "currents", etc. Their great ambition is to discuss the current—and follow it! A truly modest ambition!

However, if I am still overwhelmed with admiration for certain passages of Dante, Sophocles, and Moses, and if I feel, at certain moments, that Æschylus is closer to me than Apollinarius—if this crucial and overwhelming "experience" exists—then there must be in art a certain "invariable" of whose existence our out-and-out evolutionists have no suspicion; a certain hard and durable stony nucleus which the movements whence proceed the successive alluvia of the centuries have neither eroded nor swept away.

I know there are coxcombs who will tell you: "That's all out of date, it's in the manner of ten years, twenty years ago." When anyone speaks to you thus you can change the subject; the odds are against your being unjust to him.

Newcomers have thought to preserve their independence by substituting, for the immobile model of the ancients, the mobile model known as a "movement" or "current". They live in perpetual enslavement to their dread of missing the "last boat", which the last "current" brings and will shortly take away. In their anxiety they never stop glancing at their watch and regulating it—at the risk of putting it out of order—and in listening to its ticking they forget the beating of their hearts.

ART AND THE EPOCH

When matters have reached this stage almost the best thing to do would be to emancipate the artists, to remind them that if there is truth in the theory of the evolution of styles, there was also truth in the absolute model of Aristotle. Theoretically each of the theses has its value. Practically (or pragmatically), if we consider the repercussions of these theories on artistic creation, I am afraid the balance is not definitely in Aristotle's favour. The modernists, and above all certain ultra-modernists who push the theory of evolution to its extremest corollaries, consider that a work of art is really valuable only at the moment of its birth; a notion of which the inevitable results are haste, scamped and bungled work, and an exhibitionistic style. Hence too the dread of being outstripped, and hence *arrivisme*. Hence, in a word, yet one more invitation (among so many others) to abandon the professional conscience in art. The professional conscience, like thought, and many other old-fashioned things (out of date because they demand long and exacting labour) is relegated to the lumber-room, in the chest marked "Mythology". Here may be found all the commodities that are not shipped on the "last boat". The classic artists, with their rather ingenuous conviction that they were working for eternity, had at least the advantage of never feeling hurried; they were able to take their time, and consequently to produce honest and competent work.

But the obsession of the model (immobile or moving) is always characteristic of the herd spirit. The creator must rid himself of both obsessions. "According to Aristotle" and "of one's time" are both the devices of talent. "To be truthful" and "to be oneself" are the devices of genius.

And is not genius precisely that which takes the form of the hard and durable rock of which we were speaking? Is it not the volcanic rock that unsettles the too sensible and too predestinate series of alluvial deposits? Is not genius simply the thing that the out-and-out evolutionists have forgotten? As against their theory of the sedimentary masterpiece, I am strongly in favour of an eruptive theory.

THE MYTH OF MODERNITY

XI

It is easy to retrace the rapid progress (or more exactly, the progression) of this idea of progress (or, more modestly, of evolution) in art.

It begins in the 18th century, with the Encyclopaedists. At first it is the idea of social progress, and as yet its influence on the arts is timid and precarious. Voltaire continues to write classic tragedies while extolling Shakespeare, and while he is beginning to develop a taste for modern and exotic subjects.

Only with Romanticism does the idea become an aesthetic theory. But how sensible is the *Préface* to *Cromwell*! Its bark is worse than its bite. One does not demand of art that it should be "today's special"; one only asks it to be "Christian" and no longer "pagan"; not to be two thousand years behind the times; to move in the tradition in which we have been living since the Middle Ages, and which is in our blood.

It was after 1850 that things began to move more rapidly; here was progress that was very like a fall, for it seemed, like the latter, to be proportional to the square of time—at least! To make profession of the romantic faith was "to be of one's millennium". To make profession of the realistic faith was already "to be of one's century".

But when we approach the year 1900 we are expected to be of our decade. Then come the wars, and the post-war periods, and today one has to be up to the minute.

To be only "of the minute" is to be for the minute.

Come, come! Progress can hardly proceed much farther. And then we shall have to think once more of being creatures of eternity.

XII

"One calls poets all those who do not write in verse." This quip of Edmond Jalous' is highly significant of the state of a world in which everything is topsy-turvy. I recall, too, something that I heard Carl Spitteler say towards the close of his life: "Take

ART AND THE EPOCH

Nietzsche and myself today ; in Germany, it is Nietzsche who is regarded as the poet and I who am regarded as the philosopher. It is quite simple : Nietzsche writes in prose and I write in verse." In everything our age is lacking in measure, and never have people so excelled in inflating a little truth until they turn it into a great folly. The truth, under the circumstances, is that poetry is not essentially bound up with the form of prose. But I know more than one of our contemporaries who would be greatly surprised to learn that this has already been said by Aristotle, and said very well. It is in the ninth book of his Poetics : "For the difference between the poet and the historian is not that one speaks in verse, the other in prose ; the writings of Herodotus put into verse would still be only a history, etc. . . ." But this is not in any way sensational ; not sensational enough for our taste. We are *blasés*, in respect of the truths of common sense ; we have to have "something new" at any cost, according to the dangerous formula of the splenetic Baudelaire ; and so we take a flying leap into the absurd. But perhaps one grows tired of the absurd sooner than of common sense ; I find that reassuring.

XIII

Here is a characteristic of our epoch : the sudden metamorphosis of paradoxes into commonplaces. These vulgarized paradoxes are the *parvenus* of opinion. The wittier they were when they kept to their rôle of paradox, the more arrogant, clumsy and stupid is their behaviour henceforth ; they have all the traits of the *nouveau riche*.

XIV

Among these petty truths, inflated until they become absurd, is one whose extraordinary career has perhaps continued long enough. It is that which pretends that French poetry begins with Baudelaire ; unless indeed it begins with Lautréamont or Rimbaud. Shades of Ronsard and Villon, what do you say to this ? Say nothing : leave it to Rabelais. He will avenge you.

THE MYTH OF MODERNITY

XV

Is it presumption to assert that our generation, that we who knew war on emerging from childhood, or even in childhood, are truly "the sacrificed generation", as Charles Reber chose one day to call it ? Our misery was such that many of us had not the strength to bear it ; then they forgot it—repressed it—like those victims of concussion or shell-shock who have forgotten the shock and its circumstances. They play the buffoon ; they would like to laugh, but their laughter is more like a grinding of the teeth. But above all, our first impulse was never to forgive the men who preceded us for the disaster into which they hurled us. Then there was the demon of the post-war period, the spirit that delighted in stripping corpses, the ferocity born of war itself, which prolongs it in a more hideous form ; the cynical struggle of man against man, the evil fever that makes men trample on tombs, and on the living bodies of those who refuse to die. Of old the beardless artists honoured the old masters with a timid admiration, touching and ingenuous ; for us, we spit on them. Of old one was ashamed of not having read all the classics : as for us, we consider a puerile ignorance our surest title to glory—which is not perhaps an excellent recipe for the preservation of culture. But what does culture matter ? The only thing that matters is to get somewhere ! The art of the dirt-track is the great modern art.

XVI

It must be admitted that the present contempt for our elders, and at the same time for the tradition of culture which they endeavour to transmit to us, is not without valid excuses : the men—and the centuries—that preceded us have thrown the world, have thrown *us*, into the chaos and the ruination that we see before us ; how shall we have confidence in the fathers who have so administered the patrimony of their sons ? In a past that has created this present ? Hence the audacity of the "new youth" ; it is its mission to rebuild the world ! It is beginning today, and

ART AND THE EPOCH

all things are permissible, since one cannot do worse than has been done. Hence a naïve arrogance, which very soon becomes irritating, but behind which one can but perceive the distress from which it proceeds. Hence the disdain for all that is old (and everything is old to the young !) and the confidence reposed only in extreme youth. (Hence, for one thing, in poetry, the sudden choice of such models as the young Lautréamont, the boy Rimbaud.) As for me, I would rather have the audacity without the disdain (which after all is not so young !). This disdain fills me with anxiety, for it affords proof of a singular lack of discernment, in short, of intelligence. When we have driven off the ship of culture which the ocean of Time is seeking to bring to our shores, when we have sunk it by hurling stones at it, as urchins might stone a dog swimming for its life, when we have had a good laugh at this hooligan exploit, what will be left for us ? Shall we plunder the wreckage ?

XVII

In the heart of strongly constituted societies, closed systems in a state of equilibrium, the poet is "of his time" and does not perceive that he is so. At all events, in the past, deprived as he was of historical and other geographical landmarks, he did not realize it. For this society in which he was living was for him the world and the very order of things. Of this well-organized body the poet is the soul. Such epochs are described as classic. Then the poet is "of his time", as the fruit is proper to the season, as the song is proper to the bird.

XVIII

Where society is no longer in equilibrium, when it becomes disorganized and reverts to the chaos in which other worlds are fermenting, everything is at sixes and sevens ; and the poet also parts company with his environment. He feels then that he is no longer a part of this whole ; but this is because there is no longer a whole ; all its parts are disjoined and the great body is dislocated.

The poet parts company with the beliefs of the community. But this is because the community no longer has any beliefs; they fall from him in tatters; he does not discard them, but they desert him; as the cast-off clothes desert a beggar. He becomes a beggar. He withdraws from the morality of the community (and here we may recall the notorious prosecution of a Flaubert, a Baudelaire), but this is because the community no longer has a morality; it has only the notorious homage of vice to virtue. The poet has become a soul in distress, with all that this means in the shape of malediction. An errant soul, which sometimes tries to adapt itself in its phantom existence (symbolism!) and sometimes realizes that it must find a body again, and professes that it must be "of its time". But it professes this precisely because it is, at this juncture, impossible, because it can find no time to which it could attach itself. One theorizes only about the life one cannot lead, for if one could lead it one would do so, and would no longer think about it.

XIX

And here is this age, an age which is a mechanical bird without a bill, a bird without a song, and which does not even feel the need of a song. And the poet then is a song without a bird, a song that wanders round this bird, deprived of its voice, and around this "world without a soul". As a matter of fact he is still "of his time", he is of this world, but in the fashion of a melancholy and enchanted satellite, which influences the spirits of women and the dreams of somnambulists, and which performs honestly, even if it is unperceived, its function of lunations and tides, and sports with the tresses of the drowned. This is a fate not without grandeur: "the spirit floating on the waters."

XX

But when all is said, is it not in these times, which of all times are most inhospitable to the poet, that the poet best manifests his true function, the function of the exile, whom Plato banished

ART AND THE EPOCH

from the Republic ? Even in the best constituted societies the poet can never be satisfied with the world which he inhabits and inspires. All time, even the most harmonious, is too temporal, and the poet is a denizen of the eternal. All time is a creature drowned in the ocean of the temporal, and the poet breathes only in the eternal, in the light air which is divided from the waters. But he does not remain there, for then he would be only a sage. It is the sage who says "suave mari magno" . . . and leaves all the world to drown. But for his part, he lives, for he is a poet, he is a diving bird, and he is never so excited as by the spray. There he is to his time as the diver is to the drowning man. He brings it back to the shore, though it struggles against him. And it is during the amorous journey which brings it back that he makes the act of poetry. And this act he must always renew ; for time is always temporal, and always—more or less—drowned in the temporal.

THE END

GEORGE ALLEN & UNWIN LTD
LONDON: 40 MUSEUM STREET, W.C.1
CAPE TOWN: 58–60 LONG STREET
TORONTO: 91 WELLINGTON STREET WEST
BOMBAY: 15 GRAHAM ROAD, BALLARD ESTATE
CALCUTTA: 17 CENTRAL AVENUE, P.O. DHARAMTALA,
WELLINGTON, N.Z.: 8 KINGS CRESCENT, LOWER HUTT
SYDNEY, N.S.W.: BRADBURY HOUSE, 55 YORK STREET